GALTON BLACKISTON   A RETURN TO REAL COOKING

PHOTOGRAPHY BY **CHRIS EVERARD**

Published for Morston Hall Hotels Ltd
Morston, Holt, Norfolk NR25 7AA
Tel: 01263 741041 Fax: 01263 740419
email:reception@morstonhall.com
www.morstonhall.com

By Navigator Guides Ltd
The Old Post Office, Swanton Novers
Melton Constable, Norfolk NR24 2AJ
Tel: 01263 861141
email:info@navigatorguides.com
www.navigatorguides.com

Managing Editor: Jo Lamiri
Proofreader: Kay Worboys
Indexing: Isobel McLean
Jacket and text design: Paul Webster

ISBN 10: 1-903872-19-7
ISBN 13: 978-1-903872-19-2

A catalogue record for this book is available from the
British Library

Colour reproduction by PDQ Digital Media Solutions Ltd
Printed in Spain by Mateu Cromo

GALTON BLACKISTON
A RETURN TO REAL COOKING

ACKNOWLEDGEMENTS

Having endured torture in getting my first book completed on time, this one has gone much more smoothly. And it's been enjoyable working with a group of friends, all experts in their own fields.

I'm also grateful to my father Bill and Tracy's parents, Jan and Rogger, for their invaluable help with our children, Harry and Sam. Thanks also to our brilliant staff at Morston Hall, in particular Liz, who skilfully decodes my appalling writing and Sam and Toby in the kitchen, who maintained their good humour even when I had my 'grumpy head' on.

Although it's difficult to pick out individuals, the book would not have happened without the cajoling and occasional strops of the ever-supportive and enthusiastic Neil Alston. In addition to his own business interests, Neil helps with my food workshops. He has become a close friend of the family and is an extremely accomplished cook.

Another important contribution has come from our talented photographer, Chris Everard, whose brilliant collection of shots capture the essence of my cooking and the beauty of North Norfolk. It was also a great pleasure to work with our meticulous editor, Jo Lamiri, who made sure my recipes made sense. I even let her get her own way sometimes!

I'm also privileged to have someone of Simon Hopkinson's stature writing the foreword. He's a friend of long standing, whose work I've always rated and respected.

Also a big thank you to our marketing expert Andy Slamin, who made sure the book communicates its theme of a return to real cooking.

A large part of the success of my first book, *Cooking at Morston Hall*, was that the recipes work at home. It's been no different with this book. Special thanks to our testers – Christopher and Lynn Ball, Bill and Harry Blackiston, Kay Blackiston, Julia Buckingham, Rod Canham, Jane and Will Carter, Anne Huggins, Carol Knowles, Lois and Charlie Murphy, Sheila Parkes, Rebecca Partridge, Rosemarie Powell, Sandra and Nigel Worthington, Barbara York and Jenny Youngs.

And last, but definitely not least, I would like to thank my wife Tracy, the brains behind the business, and our two wonderful boys. I feel incredibly fortunate to have such a supportive family. Whatever success I've achieved is as much down to them as it is to me.

CONTENTS

FOREWORD

What a truly lovely book this is! And to be moved to exclaim in such a way over any cookery book in these days of almost saturation point gives me enormous pleasure.

Galton Blackiston seems to have that rare talent, these days, of being a real cook's cook, although he is also a chef and hotelier (together with his charming wife, Tracy) of long standing, with a reputation stretching far beyond Morston, the north Norfolk coast and East Anglia. His deep enthusiasm is all about making food taste as good as it possibly can; he really knows – and really cares – how his dishes will taste once they are on the plate.

I have been visiting Morston Hall for about 10 years now, mostly at Easter time. Over that period there have certainly been subtle changes in the way that Galton cooks. As the title of the book suggests, it is the time to reflect upon how his cooking has evolved – everyone's does, after all – and also how, now, much more is appreciated by those who choose to eat it.

He is passionate about his local suppliers, they being as loyal to him as he is to them, with those ingredients being employed as a seasonal joy each and every time they evolve throughout the year. So, Norfolk asparagus is teamed with early potatoes and crisp bacon; local fillets of plaice – such a delicious fish and too rarely seen in good restaurants – with tartare sauce; a 'favourite' lobster salad; Morston crab cakes; prawn bisque. This last recipe, the bisque, truly thrills me as it is made from discarded prawn shells (presumably left over from making the cocktail), stewed into a rich broth and pulverised to a super-smooth kitchen classic. And, as Galton makes quite clear, this is something so very easily done in the home. How good it makes one feel that here is someone who is telling you how to make something from ingredients that usually end up in the bin. The sign of a special cook, to be sure.

Galton Blackiston's new cookery book is one to be thoroughly used. Its pages should soon be stuck together with ease.

Simon Hopkinson

INTRODUCTION

So what exactly do I mean by a return to real cooking? For me, real cooking involves using locally sourced, seasonal ingredients of the highest quality and cooking them as simply as possible. It's simple things done well rather than complicated things done badly that really interests me.

Over the last couple of decades, with our increasingly busy lifestyles, these traditional skills seem somehow to have been lost. And so, in turn, our children have had little chance to learn real cooking skills from their parents.

What's more, we live in an age when most fruit and vegetables can be bought regardless of whether they are in season or not. And yet to get the best flavours from a meal it's so important to use ingredients that are fresh and in season.

Fortunately, there seems to be a growing trend back towards using locally grown, fresh produce, allowing the natural flavour and goodness in the ingredients to shine through. This is my 'mantra' and I hope this book will provide you with exciting ideas simply by combining the right ingredients and some simple instructions!

When I analyse how my own style of cooking has changed over the 15 years that Tracy and I have been running Morston Hall, it's quite an eye opener. In hindsight some of my early menus were too complicated – fussy dishes to which I added ingredients simply because they were there. Nowadays I deliberately leave things out of a dish to allow the main ingredient to shine. For example, I prefer to roast pheasant in the traditional way, carved thinly at the table and served with bread sauce, crisp bacon, game chips, fried breadcrumbs and gravy made from the roasting tin. This is real cooking – and a theme that runs throughout the recipes in the book.

Another important aspect of this book is that I am confident the recipes will work at home. Preparing food in a commercial environment and in the kitchen at home are hugely different experiences, which is why every one of these recipes has been tested by friends and family (with huge enthusiasm!) in their own homes, without them telephoning me when problems arose. We took note of their comments and, where appropriate, adjusted the recipes for home use. It is with real gratitude that I thank all our testers – their feedback was invaluable. What's more, many of the recipes can be prepared partly or wholly in advance, which is a bonus for hassle-free entertaining.

Please make sure you read the recipes right through before cooking them and don't be frightened to substitute if you need to: if the recipe says use a shallot and you only have a small onion, that's fine. Likewise, if you have some chicken stock, rather than beef stock, use that instead. I have made every effort not to use weird and wonderful ingredients that are hard to track down.

I hope you enjoy the book and share my passion for a return to real cooking.

Galton Blackiston

IN THE KITCHEN

Breads

t's amazing how things have changed during the fifteen years we have been at Morston. When we first opened we did one type of bread for dinner and wholemeal bread for breakfast toast. But in our business we have to strive to improve all the time, which is why we now offer three different types of bread or rolls every evening, as well as sultana and walnut bread with cheese.

Bread-making at home is very therapeutic and literally 'hands on', allowing you to feel the dough during the kneading process, which is why I am keen to encourage you to have a go at making your own. You'll also discover how easy it is: although it takes about 2 hours from start to finish, you can get on with other jobs while it's proving. In any case, as I always say, you do need to set aside time for cooking if you're going to do it properly.

The bread recipes in this chapter all work well in their own right, but you should also experiment with other fillings. One thing I am strict about, though, is the method of making bread, and choose to make mine in a food mixer. At cookery demonstrations I am often asked whether my breads can be made in a breadmaker: I don't know the answer to this question as I have never used one, mainly because they demand dried yeast and I have only ever used fresh yeast to make bread because it gives a better result. (Moreover, fresh yeast is the yeast of choice for every baker in the land!) You can find it at the fresh bread counter in supermarkets.

One tip when making bread is to make sure the liquid ingredients are always lukewarm (but err on the side of caution: better too cool than too hot), as this will help the yeast to ferment. In the summertime, we often make bread with cold, sparkling water otherwise it proves too quickly in a hot kitchen. You can, if you're feeling purist, also warm the bowl of the food mixer. In the recipes I suggest allowing the machine to knead the dough for 5-8 minutes, but you can leave it for longer.

Pastry recipes also appear in this chapter. As with breads, pastry-making at Morston has moved on, and we now make quite a few different pastries, all by hand. I realise that many people buy ready-made pastry, but home-made is streets ahead and well worth the effort.

I think you need a light touch when making scones and shortcrust pastry. Many types of pastry – particularly those with a high fat content – can be made just as successfully in a food processor.

People often ask me if breads and pastry can be frozen. The good news for busy cooks is that they can. Pastry will keep in the fridge for two to three days but is best frozen if you're keeping it for longer than that. Breads, on the other hand, should be frozen as soon as they are cool.

Almond Shortbread Biscuits

You'll find plenty of uses for these moreish little biscuits: I like them as an accompaniment to fruit fool and as an integral part of Peach Melba (*see* page 212). I also use the pastry for lining flan rings for sweet tarts – Amaretti biscuits give the pastry a really distinctive flavour. The pastry can be made in a food processor, using the pulse action, although at Morston we prefer to make it by hand.

Makes about 40 biscuits

225g (8oz) soft plain flour, sifted, plus extra for rolling

50g (2oz) Amaretti biscuits, finely ground in a food processor

75g (3oz) golden caster sugar

a good pinch of salt

175g (6oz) unsalted butter, softened

1 egg yolk

2 tbsp milk

In a large bowl, combine the flour, Amaretti biscuits, sugar and salt. Cut the butter into knobs and, using your fingertips, rub it into the flour mixture until well incorporated.

Mix the egg yolk and milk together, then add to the bowl, binding the mixture together with your fingertips until the pastry comes together. Divide into 2 equal balls, wrap in clingfilm and chill for at least 1 hour.

When ready to use the pastry, remove from the fridge and work it with your hands until it becomes soft and pliable. Then, on a lightly floured surface, roll the pastry out as thinly as you dare. Using a round, 5cm (2 inch) cutter, cut out the biscuits and place them on a greaseproof paper-covered baking tray.

Pre-heat the oven to 180C/350F/Gas 4.

Bake the biscuits in the centre of the oven for about 10 minutes until lightly golden. Remove from the oven and place on a wire rack to cool. These biscuits will keep for several days in an airtight container.

Bacon and Onion Bread

Every day in the kitchen at Morston we make two or three types of bread – this wonderful, delicious, full-flavoured bread is one of the more recent additions to our ever-increasing repertoire. For the best flavour, use really good smoked streaky bacon.

Makes 2 large loaves or 30 rolls

10g (½oz) lard

110g (4oz) good-quality smoked streaky bacon, finely chopped

4 shallots, peeled and finely chopped

700g (1½lb) strong plain flour

1 tsp salt

1 tsp mustard powder

55ml (2fl oz) olive oil

25g (1oz) fresh yeast

1 tsp caster sugar

150ml (¼ pint) lukewarm milk

1 egg, beaten

150ml (¼ pint) lukewarm water

Melt the lard in a frying pan. Fry the bacon until well-coloured and crisp, then drain it on kitchen paper. In the remaining fat, fry the shallots until soft, then mix them in a bowl with the bacon. Set aside to cool.

Place the flour, salt, mustard powder and olive oil in the bowl of a food mixer. Add the cooled bacon and shallots. Using the dough hook, mix thoroughly.

Combine the yeast and sugar in a bowl. Mix with your fingertips so that the yeast breaks down and becomes smooth and almost liquid.

Add the milk, beaten egg and water, then mix thoroughly. With the machine still running, slowly add this mixture to the flour (you may not need to use all of the liquid), then allow the machine to knead the dough for 5-8 minutes, or until it comes away from the sides of the bowl and does not stick to your fingers.

Remove the bowl from the mixer and cover the dough with a clean, damp tea towel. Leave in a warm place for about 1 hour, or until the dough has doubled in volume.

Turn the dough out on to a lightly floured surface. Knead well with the palm of your hand, then divide into 2 equal-sized loaves. Place them on a large, greaseproof paper-covered baking tray, leaving plenty of room for the dough to rise again, and leave for at least 40 minutes.

Pre-heat the oven to 220C/425F/Gas 7.

Once the dough has doubled in size again, place in the centre of the pre-heated oven and bake for 20-25 minutes until golden: it should sound hollow when you tap your knuckles on the tops of the loaves.

Remove from the oven and leave to cool.

Bread with Anchovies, Caperberries and Lemon

This is a really good bread for 'mopping up' juices from your plate, especially anything that involves roasted peppers and tomatoes. Instead of spreading this bread with butter, I prefer to douse it liberally with olive oil as it comes out of the oven. I use the large plumper caperberries with stalks still attached, but if you cannot find them, ordinary capers will do.

Makes 1 loaf

275g (10oz) strong plain flour, plus extra for kneading

a good pinch of salt

zest of ½ lemon, finely grated

25g (1oz) butter, softened

1 clove of garlic, peeled and finely grated

10g (½oz) fresh yeast

1 tsp caster sugar

1 egg, beaten

150ml (¼ pint) lukewarm milk

1 small tin of anchovies, halved crossways

1 small jar of caperberries

olive oil for dousing

Place the flour, salt, lemon zest, butter and garlic in the bowl of a food mixer and, using the dough hook, mix thoroughly.

Combine the yeast and sugar in a bowl. Mix with your fingertips so that the yeast breaks down and becomes smooth and almost liquid. Add the egg and the milk and mix this together well.

With the machine still running, slowly add this mixture to the flour (you may not need to use all of the liquid). Allow the machine to knead the dough for 5-8 minutes, or until it comes away from the sides of the bowl and does not stick to your fingers.

Remove the bowl from the mixer and cover the dough with a clean, damp tea towel. Leave in a warm place for about 1 hour, or until the dough has doubled in volume.

Turn the dough out on to a lightly floured surface, knead well with the palm of your hand, then shape the dough into 1 large loaf. Place it on a large, greaseproof paper-covered baking tray, leaving enough room for the dough to rise again.

Using your forefinger, make indentations in the dough at 1cm (½ inch) intervals and push a piece of anchovy and a caperberry right in to the bottom of each one. Liberally drizzle the top of the loaf with olive oil and leave the dough in a warm place for a further 45 minutes.

Pre-heat the oven to 220C/425F/Gas 7.

Once the dough has proved and doubled in size again, place it in the centre of the pre-heated oven and bake for 20-25 minutes until golden: it should sound hollow when you tap your knuckles on the top of the loaf. Remove from the oven and leave to cool.

Just before serving, re-heat the bread at 200C/400F/Gas 6 for 5 minutes. Drizzle the top with more olive oil, slice the bread thickly and serve warm.

Classic Pastry

For me, there is great satisfaction in making pastry by hand. The flavour and texture is infinitely better than any bought pastry I have tasted, so go on, back into the kitchen and make your own! It goes against the grain for me to admit this, but pastry can be made very successfully in a food processor. These recipes for savoury shortcrust pastry (pâte brisée) and sweet shortcrust pastry (pâte sucrée) each make enough to line two 23cm (9 inch) flan rings, so you can use half and freeze the other half (shaped flat or into a sausage for quicker thawing). When you take pastry from the fridge, really work it with your hands to make it pliable and easier to roll thinly.

Savoury Pastry (Pâte Brisée)

Makes enough to
line two 23cm
(9 inch) flan rings

250g (9oz) plain flour

a good pinch of salt

1 tsp icing sugar

50g (2oz) lard

75g (3oz) salted butter,
  softened

1 egg, lightly beaten with
  3 tbsp milk

Place the flour, salt, sugar, lard and butter in a large bowl and, using your fingertips, mix them together until they resemble fine breadcrumbs. Add the beaten egg and milk, then bring the pastry together.

Turn it out on to a very lightly floured surface. Divide the pastry in two, wrap in clingfilm and place in the fridge for at least 1 hour before using. (The pastry can also be made ahead and kept in the fridge for up to 4 days, or frozen.)

Sweet Pastry (Pâte Sucrée)

Makes enough to
line two 23cm
(9 inch) flan rings

250g (9oz) plain flour

75g (3oz) caster sugar

pinch of salt

the seeds from 1 vanilla pod

150g (5oz) unsalted butter,
  softened

1 egg, lightly beaten with
  1 tbsp milk

Place the flour, sugar, salt, vanilla seeds and butter in the bowl of a food processor and, using the pulse action, whiz briefly to combine.

Add the beaten egg and milk, then process again until the pastry comes together and leaves the sides of the bowl.

Turn it out on to a very lightly floured surface. Divide the pastry in two, wrap in clingfilm and place in the fridge for at least 1 hour before using. (The pastry can also be made ahead and kept in the fridge for up to 4 days, or frozen.)

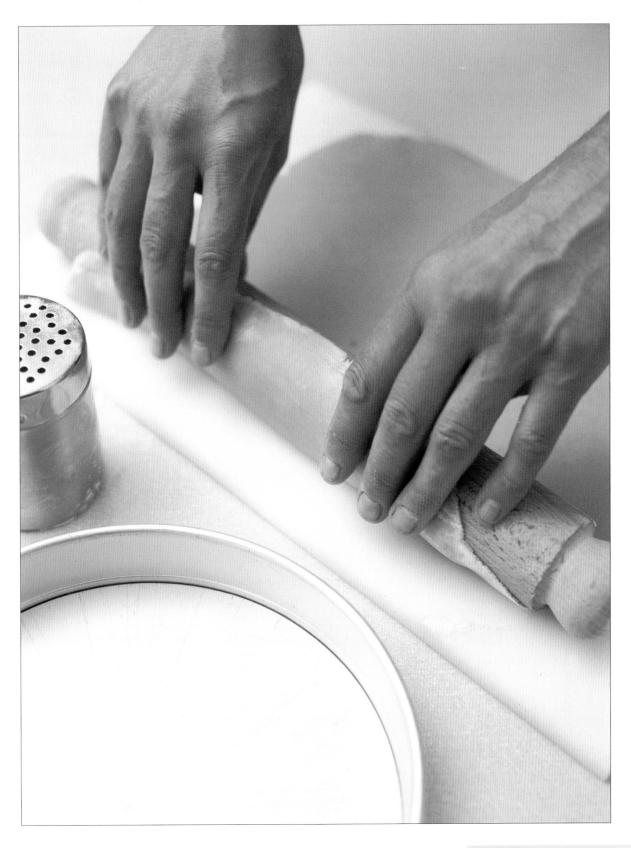

Crisp Cheddar Biscuits

These little biscuits make great canapé bases or are just very good with a plate of cheese. The pastry also freezes well.

Makes about 40
biscuits

Makes about 40
biscuits

150g (5oz) plain flour, plus

extra for rolling

a good pinch of paprika

110g (4oz) unsalted butter,

softened

110g (4oz) mature Cheddar,

finely grated

Place all the ingredients in the bowl of a food processor. Using the pulse action, combine them until they come away from the sides of the bowl. Remove from the processor and, using your hands, bring the pastry together on a lightly floured surface. Wrap the pastry in clingfilm and chill for 1 hour.

Pre-heat the oven to 170C/325F/Gas 3.

When you are ready to make the biscuits, mould the dough in your hands until soft and pliable, then roll it out on a lightly floured surface. Using a 5cm (2 inch) plain pastry cutter, cut out about 40 little round biscuits.

Place the biscuits on a baking tray and bake in the centre of the pre-heated oven for about 20 minutes, or until lightly golden. Remove from the oven and cool on a wire rack before storing in an airtight container.

Garlic Rolls

Once, when we had a lot of bread rolls left over, rather than waste them, we turned them into garlic rolls, which are now one of our most popular breads. You can take the rolls to the table still wrapped in foil – as your guests open them, the wonderful aroma escapes.

**Makes 16 rolls or
2 large loaves**

450g (1lb) strong plain flour,
   plus extra for kneading

a good pinch of salt

25g (1oz) salted butter,
   softened

20g (¾oz) fresh yeast

1 tsp caster sugar

120ml (4fl oz) lukewarm
   water

1 egg, beaten

120ml (4fl oz) lukewarm milk

For the garlic butter

110g (4oz) salted butter

2 cloves of garlic, peeled and
   finely chopped

1 tbsp each snipped chives,
   chopped parsley, tarragon
   and mint

Place the flour, a good pinch of salt and the butter in the bowl of a food mixer and, using the dough hook, mix thoroughly.

Combine the yeast and sugar in a bowl. Mix with your fingertips so that the yeast breaks down and becomes smooth and almost liquid. Add the warm water, egg and milk, then mix together thoroughly.

With the machine still running, slowly add this mixture to the flour (you may not need to use all of the liquid). Allow the machine to knead the dough for 5-8 minutes, or until it comes away from the sides of the bowl and does not stick to your fingers.

Remove the bowl from the mixer and cover the dough with a clean, damp tea towel. Leave in a warm place for about 1 hour, or until the dough has doubled in volume.

Turn the dough out on to a lightly floured surface, knead well with the palm of your hand, then divide it into 16 equal-sized pieces. Using the palm of your hand, roll them on a lightly floured surface into round rolls. Place the rolls on to a large, greaseproof paper-covered baking tray, leaving plenty of room for the dough to rise again. Leave in a warm place until the dough has doubled in size.

Pre-heat the oven to 220C/425F/Gas 7.

Meanwhile, make up the garlic and herb butter. Melt the butter in a small saucepan over a very gentle heat. Off the heat, add the garlic followed by the herbs and mix well. Set aside.

Place the risen rolls in the pre-heated oven and bake for 20-25 minutes until golden brown; when you tap the rolls, they should sound hollow.

Leave the rolls to cool slightly then, using a sharp, serrated knife, slice deeply at 1cm (½ inch) intervals, making about 4 slices in each roll, but without cutting all the way through. Liberally brush each cut surface with garlic butter before wrapping each roll in foil. Re-heat for about 10 minutes in the oven at 200C/400F/Gas 6.

Hot Cross Buns

Things don't get much better than a warmed hot cross bun with plenty of butter, clotted cream and jam! At Easter, we serve these every morning from Good Friday through to the following Tuesday. Any left over are toasted and served at teatime with a good wedge of simnel cake. They do keep fairly well in an airtight container – a bonus if you have a large family gathering over the holiday period – but are best made and eaten on the same day.

Makes 16-18

For the rolls

450g (1lb) strong plain flour, plus extra for kneading

a good pinch of salt

75g (3oz) butter, softened

20g (¾oz) fresh yeast

40g (1½oz) caster sugar

120ml (4fl oz) lukewarm water

1 egg, beaten

120ml (4fl oz) lukewarm milk

150g (5oz) mixed dried fruits, such as sultanas, currants and mixed peel

½ tsp ground nutmeg

½ tsp ground cinnamon

For the crosses

4 tbsp plain flour

1 tbsp caster sugar

3 tbsp cold water

For the glaze

3 tbsp sugar

3 tbsp lukewarm water

Place the flour, a good pinch of salt and the butter in the bowl of a food mixer and, using the dough hook, mix thoroughly.

Combine the yeast and sugar in a bowl. Mix with your fingertips so that the yeast breaks down and becomes smooth and almost liquid. Add the warm water, egg and milk, then mix together thoroughly.

Take about 25g (1oz) of the flour mixture and add this to the yeast liquid. Whisk well and set aside for about 10 minutes, by which time the yeast should have frothed up.

In the meantime, add the mixed fruits and spices to the remaining flour in the mixer and slowly mix together.

With the machine still running, slowly add the yeast mixture to the flour. Allow the machine to knead the mixture for 5-8 minutes, or until it comes away from the sides of the bowl. Remove the bowl from the mixer and cover the dough with a clean, damp tea towel. Leave in a warm place for about 1 hour, or until the dough has doubled in size.

Turn the dough out on to a lightly floured work surface, knead well with the palm of your hand and then divide into 16-18 equal-sized buns. Place on a large, flat greaseproof paper-covered baking tray, making sure they have enough room to expand. Leave them, uncovered, in a warm place to double in size again.

Pre-heat the oven to 200C/400F/Gas 6.

While the buns are proving, make up the mixture for the crosses by mixing all the ingredients in a bowl to form a thick paste. Place this in a small piping bag (you can make one out of a triangle of greaseproof paper).

When the dough has risen, quickly pipe crosses over the top and bake the buns in the centre of the oven for about 20 minutes until they are a deep golden colour.

Meanwhile, make the glaze by dissolving the sugar in the water.

Remove the buns from the oven and, while still hot, brush the glaze over each one. Serve warm.

Mozzarella, Basil and Fig Bread

Mozzarella, basil and figs combine so well in a salad that they were the inspiration for this wonderful bread. Its mild cheese and basil flavour has proved very popular with guests, especially in the summer. I buy most of my flour from Letheringsett Mill, a local water-powered mill. Their flour is distributed nationwide and to many London chefs.

Makes 2 loaves

570g (1¼lb) strong plain
  flour, plus extra for
  kneading

1 level tsp salt

50g (2oz) softened butter

25g (1oz) fresh yeast

1 level tsp caster sugar

150ml (¼ pint) lukewarm
  water

1 egg

150ml (¼ pint) milk

275g (10oz) mozzarella
  cheese, cut into 1cm
  (½ inch) cubes

4 black figs, cut into
  quarters then halved

about 35 leaves of fresh
  basil

several good slugs of
  olive oil

sea salt flakes

Place the flour, salt and butter in the bowl of a food mixer and, using the dough hook, mix thoroughly.

Combine the yeast and sugar in a bowl. Mix with your fingertips so that the yeast breaks down and becomes smooth and almost liquid. Add the warm water, egg and milk, then mix thoroughly.

With the machine still running, slowly add this mixture to the flour (you may not need to use all of the liquid). Knead the dough for 5-8 minutes, or until it comes away from the sides of the bowl and does not stick to your fingers.

Remove the bowl from the mixer and cover the dough with a clean, damp tea towel. Leave in a warm place for about 1 hour, or until the dough has doubled in volume.

Turn the dough out on to a lightly floured surface, knead well with the palm of your hand then divide the dough into 2 equal-sized loaves. Place these on a large, greaseproof paper-covered baking tray, leaving enough room for the dough to prove again.

Using your forefinger, make indentations in the dough at 2.5cm (1 inch) intervals and push a piece of mozzarella and fig rolled up in a basil leaf right in to the bottom of each one. Liberally drizzle the top of the loaves with olive oil, and sprinkle with flakes of sea salt. Leave the dough to prove and double in size again for a further 45 minutes in a warm place.

Pre-heat the oven to 220C/425F/Gas 7.

Once the dough has doubled in size again, place it in the centre of the pre-heated oven and bake for 20-25 minutes until golden: they should sound hollow when you tap your knuckles on the tops of the loaves. Allow to cool.

Just before serving, re-heat the bread in an oven at 200C/400F/Gas 6 for 5 minutes. Drizzle the top with more olive oil, slice the bread thickly and serve warm.

Neil's Fruit Cake

I don't think I've tasted a better fruit cake than this one from my very good friend Neil Alston – without whom this book would not have seen the light of day. Neil is a very good cook in his own right and this cake is testimony to his talents. I reckon that very slow cooking contributes to the success of this recipe; Neil cooks it in his Aga, but we have tested and adapted it for a conventional oven. You'll find the cake keeps well for around two months.

For a 20cm (8 inch) deep-sided square cake tin

175g (6oz) naturally coloured glacé cherries

625g (1lb 6oz) currants

225g (8oz) sultanas

225g (8oz) raisins

110g (4oz) chopped mixed peel

6 tbsp brandy

400g (14oz) plain flour

½ tsp ground nutmeg

1 tsp mixed spice

350g (12oz) unsalted butter, softened

350g (12oz) dark muscovado sugar

6 eggs, lightly beaten

110g (4oz) chopped almonds

zest of 1 orange

zest of 1 lemon

1 tbsp black treacle

Start by preparing the fruit a day in advance. Rinse the glacé cherries, dry them and cut into quarters. Place all the fruit and the mixed peel in a large bowl and pour over the brandy. Mix well, then cover with clingfilm and set aside overnight.

Line the base and sides of the cake tin with baking parchment, then tie a collar of 4 layers of newspaper, wide enough to stand about 5cm (2 inches) above the rim, around the outside of the tin.

Pre-heat the oven to 120C/250F/Gas ½.

Sift the flour, nutmeg and mixed spice into a bowl. Place the butter and sugar in a food mixer and whisk thoroughly until light and fluffy.

With the food mixer still running, slowly add a little of the beaten egg. Turn off the machine, then sift in some of the flour. Repeat this process until all the egg and flour have been thoroughly whisked in.

Change the attachment on the food mixer from the whisk to the K beater. Then, on a slow speed, carefully add all the mixed, soaked fruit and peel, chopped almonds and orange and lemon zests, followed by the black treacle, until thoroughly combined.

Spoon the mixture into the prepared cake tin. Make a slight depression in the centre of the cake, then cut a small hole in the centre of a sheet of greaseproof paper and lay this on top of the raised newspaper collar.

Bake the cake in the centre of the oven for 3 hours, then turn it around and cook for a further 3 hours. After 5½ hours, start to test it every 10 minutes, until a fine skewer comes out clean when inserted into the centre of the cake. Leave it to cool. To store, wrap well in greaseproof paper and feed regularly with brandy.

Parmesan Crisps

I guarantee these little biscuits won't hang around for long! At Morston we serve them with little shot glasses of soup: they are especially good with Chilled Tomato Consommé (*see* page 48). I use a 9cm (3½ inch) pastry cutter, but you can make them smaller if you prefer. It is difficult to give an exact cooking time as oven temperatures vary – watch them carefully as they need to be golden so that they crisp up, but are also thin and delicate enough to burn easily.

**Makes about
24 crisps**

225g (8oz) fresh Parmesan,
  finely grated (you can use a
  food processor to do this)

9cm (3½ inch) plain pastry
cutter

Pre-heat the oven to 180C/350F/Gas 4.

Place the pastry cutter on a baking tray covered with greaseproof paper. Take a generous tablespoonful of grated Parmesan, scatter it inside the pastry cutter, then firm it down using the back of the spoon.

Carefully lift off the cutter and repeat this process until you have used all the Parmesan.

Place the baking tray in the centre of the pre-heated oven and bake for 8–9 minutes (you're looking for a lightly coloured crisp).

Remove from the oven and cool on a wire rack before carefully storing in an airtight container.

Savoury Muffins

Sometimes I get the urge to make my own muffins – they taste infinitely better than bought ones and are a great choice, sliced and toasted, for breakfast or teatime. If you do not have a griddle pan use a heavy-based frying pan. The important thing to remember when cooking muffins is that they must be cooked very slowly over a really low heat.

Makes about 12 muffins

350g (12oz) strong plain flour

110g (4oz) soft plain flour

a good pinch of salt

10g (½oz) fresh yeast

1 tsp caster sugar

150ml (¼ pint) lukewarm milk

150ml (¼ pint) lukewarm water

a little rice flour or ordinary strong flour for dusting (optional)

a griddle pan or very heavy-based frying pan

Place the flours and salt in the bowl of a food mixer and, using a dough hook, mix thoroughly.

Combine the yeast and the sugar in a bowl. Mix with your fingertips so that the yeast breaks down and becomes smooth and almost liquid. Add the warm milk and water.

With the machine still running, slowly add this mixture to the flour (you may not need to use all of the liquid). Allow the machine to knead the dough for 5-8 minutes, or until it comes away from the sides of the bowl and does not stick to your fingers.

Remove the bowl from the mixer and cover the dough with a clean, damp tea towel. Leave in a warm place for about 1 hour, or until the dough has doubled in volume.

Turn the dough out on to a lightly floured work surface, knead well with the palm of your hand before dividing it into 12 equal-sized pieces. Shape each piece into a small roll, then place them on a large, greaseproof paper-covered baking tray, leaving plenty of room for them to expand.

Dust the tops with a little rice flour, then place a sheet of greaseproof paper on top. Place another baking sheet on top of the paper to flatten the dough into a muffin shape. Leave for about half an hour, so that the dough proves outwards rather than upwards. (You may find you need to do this using 2 baking trays with 6 muffins on each one.)

Gently heat a griddle, without allowing it to become too hot or it will burn the muffins (as soon as you can feel the heat coming off the griddle, it is hot enough).

Cook the muffins in batches of 3, for about 8 minutes on each side until golden. Place them on a cooling rack covered with a dry cloth and, when completely cold, store in an airtight container.

Tomato and Roquefort Bread

This is probably my favourite of all the breads we make at the moment – it certainly does not need any butter serving with it. The flavours work together really well.

350g (12oz) strong plain
  flour

1 tbsp salt

1 tsp English mustard
  powder

40ml (1½fl oz) olive oil, plus
  extra for drizzling

10g (½oz) fresh yeast

1 level tsp caster sugar

75ml (3fl oz) lukewarm milk

75ml (3fl oz) lukewarm
  water

1 egg, beaten

110g (4oz) cherry vine
  tomatoes

75g (3oz) Roquefort cheese,
  cut into 1cm (½ inch)
  pieces

sea salt and pepper

Place the flour, salt, mustard powder and olive oil in the bowl of a food mixer and, using the dough hook, mix thoroughly.

Combine the yeast and sugar in a bowl. Mix with your fingertips so that the yeast breaks down and becomes smooth and almost liquid. Add the warm milk, water and egg, then mix thoroughly.

With the machine still running, slowly add this mixture to the flour (you may not need to use all of the liquid). Allow the machine to knead the dough for 5-8 minutes, or until it comes away from the sides of the bowl and does not stick to your fingers.

Remove the bowl from the mixer and cover the dough with a clean, damp tea towel. Leave in a warm place for about 1 hour, or until the dough has doubled in volume.

Turn the dough out on to a lightly floured surface, knead well with the palm of your hand, then shape the dough into 1 large loaf. Place it on a large, greaseproof paper-covered baking tray.

Using your forefinger, make indentations in the dough at 2.5cm (1 inch) intervals and push a piece of the Roquefort cheese and a cherry tomato (you may need to halve the tomatoes) right in to the bottom of each one. Liberally drizzle the top of the loaf with olive oil and sprinkle with flakes of sea salt and a good grinding of black pepper. Leave the dough to prove and double in size again for a further 45 minutes in a warm place.

Pre-heat the oven to 220C/425F/Gas 7.

Once the dough has doubled in size again, place it in the centre of the pre-heated oven and bake for 20-25 minutes until golden: it should sound hollow when you tap your knuckles on the top of the loaf. Allow to cool.

Just before serving, re-heat the bread in the oven at 200C/400F/Gas 6 for about 5 minutes. Drizzle with more olive oil, slice the bread thickly and serve while still warm.

Soups & Sauces

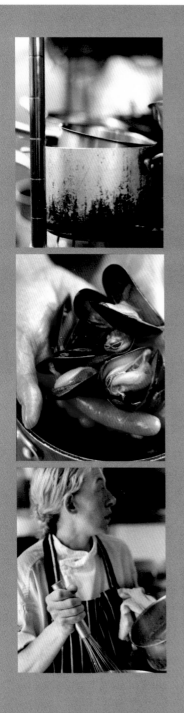

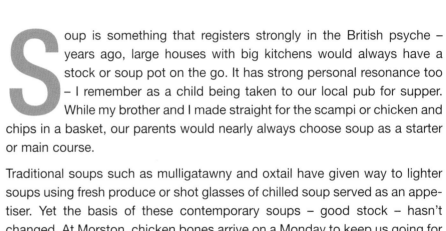

Soup is something that registers strongly in the British psyche – years ago, large houses with big kitchens would always have a stock or soup pot on the go. It has strong personal resonance too – I remember as a child being taken to our local pub for supper. While my brother and I made straight for the scampi or chicken and chips in a basket, our parents would nearly always choose soup as a starter or main course.

Traditional soups such as mulligatawny and oxtail have given way to lighter soups using fresh produce or shot glasses of chilled soup served as an appetiser. Yet the basis of these contemporary soups – good stock – hasn't changed. At Morston, chicken bones arrive on a Monday to keep us going for the week and a further consignment arrive on Thursday, which are used to make white stock for the weekend. This means we always have a pot of stock – the essential ingredient for a good kitchen – bubbling away gently, providing the base for all our gravy, soups and some of our sauces.

The downside of serving soup is that you can easily become too full to enjoy the rest of the meal, which is why our fixed menu at Morston features it as an appetiser, aiming for a small quantity of really intensely flavoured soup, giving the diner the pleasure of its intense flavour without spoiling the appetite. I also prefer to let the ingredients' flavours shine through rather than overpowering the soup with stock that is too strong.

For home cooks, the big advantage of serving soup is that it can be prepared in advance, or even frozen. However, if a soup contains cream, I would suggest adding this only when the soup has thawed and is about to be served.

Good sauces are also very important to me. My 'mantra' has always been to buy only the best-quality meat, fish, fowl or vegetables (the better your ingredients, the less you need to do to them) then cook them really simply and quickly. Cooked this way, you need add only a small amount of a really flavourful sauce – especially if it's a rich one containing butter – to complete the dish. One of the most useful all-round sauces is hollandaise, as you can make it a little ahead of serving, keeping it warm in a Thermos or bain marie. Always add herbs to sauces at the last minute and remember that a sauce is there to enhance a dish, not to overpower it, something that hadn't registered in my early days at Miller Howe when, to raised eyebrows from the guests, we once served roast loin of pork with coffee cream sauce!

Chilled Tomato Consommé

Writing for *The Independent*, the journalist and broadcaster Richard Johnson gave us a glowing report a few years ago in which he said he would have liked to lick his plate clean! He did, however, also comment that the tomato consommé lacked the sunshine of a tomato soup from Italy and he was quite right: we used tomatoes from our own greenhouse when, in fact, you need really ripe, red Italian or Spanish tomatoes bursting with flavour. Serve this highly flavoured soup chilled in a small glass as an *amuse-gueule*, maybe adding some skinned whole cherry tomatoes to serve. Your guests will be amazed that such a clear-looking soup can taste so intensely of tomatoes!

Serves 6

1kg (2lb 4oz) really ripe
  cherry vine tomatoes, taken
  off the stalk and halved

3 shallots, peeled and
  chopped

25g (1oz) fresh basil, plus
  extra freshly torn basil
  leaves, to serve

25ml (1fl oz) olive oil

½ cucumber, peeled, halved
  and deseeded

1 tsp caster sugar

salt and pepper

1 egg white and sea salt
  flakes, to serve (optional)

Place all the ingredients except for the torn basil in the bowl of a food processor. Season really well with salt and pepper (this helps to extract the juices from the tomatoes and cucumber), then whiz on a high speed.

Once the mixture is really well processed, pour it into a jelly bag or a large piece of muslin suspended over a bowl. Tie up securely and leave for 4 hours in a cool place, or until all the juices have dripped through.

Chill the consommé until ready to serve. Dip your finger into some egg white. Run it round the rim of each glass, then dip the glasses into sea salt flakes. Serve the consommé with finely torn basil sprinkled on top.

Cockle Chowder

This chowder brings back many childhood memories of time spent near Blakeney Point, bottom in the air and fingers clawing at the sand for Stiffkey Blues (local cockles with distinctive, dark blue shells). The tradition has continued and I still enjoy going out looking for cockles with our two boys, Harry and Sam. Cockles in their shells need to be thoroughly cleaned in plenty of cold, running water, then preferably left overnight in the fridge in a bowl of cold, lightly salted water with some plain flour sprinkled over the top (ingesting this flour will encourage the cockles to spit out any sand and dirt).

Serves 6

1kg (2lb 4oz) cockles in
  shells

2 tbsp olive oil

2 large shallots, peeled and
  thinly sliced

2 cloves of garlic, peeled and
  finely chopped

175ml (6fl oz) dry white wine

275ml (½ pint) whipping
  cream

25g (1oz) unsalted butter

2 red chillies, deseeded and
  finely chopped

1 lobe of fresh ginger,
  peeled and grated to give
  1 rounded tsp

4 tbsp finely chopped
  flat-leaf parsley

salt and freshly ground black
  pepper

crusty bread, to serve

Drain the cockles in a colander then leave under cold, running water for a few minutes to get rid of the flour (see intro). Heat the oil in a large pan over a medium heat, add the shallots and garlic, and fry until just starting to colour. Turn up the heat and, when the pan is really hot, shoot the cockles in and give them a good shake. Add the white wine, cover and cook over a high heat for a few minutes until the cockles have opened, then take off the heat.

Once the cockles are cool enough to handle, remove them from the shells and set them aside in a bowl, discarding any that have not opened. Strain the cooking liquor through a muslin cloth into a large bowl and reserve.

When you are ready to serve the soup, heat the reserved liquor and simmer to reduce slightly. Add the cream and reduce again, then season to taste. Five minutes before serving, add the cockles and turn the heat down to warm them through. Finally, whisk in the butter, then stir in the chillies, ginger and parsley. Serve with crusty bread.

Creamy Jerusalem Artichoke Soup

One of my favourites for late autumn or winter, this soup is much lighter than the original which, according to my mother, "looked like death and tasted like death." It also freezes well, but don't add the cream till you are ready to serve it. Try to use English onions for this recipe as they have a much stronger flavour.

Serves 8

50g (2oz) salted butter

3 medium English onions, peeled and thinly sliced

900g (2lb) Jerusalem artichokes, peeled and chopped

850ml (1½ pints) chicken stock

juice of 1 lemon

150ml (¼ pint) double cream

white truffle oil (optional)

salt and pepper

Heat a large saucepan, then add the butter. When it has melted, stir in the sliced onions and cook until translucent. Add the artichokes and enough chicken stock to cover, then bring to the boil. Turn down the heat, add the lemon juice and cover the artichokes with a layer of greaseproof paper. Cook them gently for 20-25 minutes until the artichokes have softened.

Blitz the contents of the pan in a liquidiser until smooth, then strain through a fine sieve into a clean saucepan.

When you are ready to serve, gently reheat the soup. Stir in the cream, adjust the seasoning and ladle into warmed bowls. For extra indulgence, drizzle a few drops of white truffle oil over before serving.

Lightly Curried Parsnip and Apple Soup

The longer you liquidise this soup, the creamier it will become, which also makes it much easier to pass through a sieve. I tend to liquidise a small batch at a time, covering the top of the machine with a tea towel to stop any liquid exploding out of the top! You can make this soup more substantial by serving it with some lightly poached smoked haddock; I also like to float a teaspoon of apple purée on top of the soup.

Serves 6

50g (2oz) butter

2 medium onions, peeled
and finely sliced

500g (1lb 2oz) parsnips,
peeled and finely sliced

1 Bramley apple, about 175g
(6oz), peeled, cored and
finely chopped

850ml (1½ pints) chicken or
vegetable stock

1 generous tbsp mild curry
powder

150ml (¼ pint) whipping
cream

salt and pepper

Melt the butter in a large saucepan, then add the onions and sweat them until soft. Add the parsnips, apple and stock and simmer for about 20 minutes until the parsnips are softened.

Stir in the curry powder followed by the cream and allow to bubble for a couple of minutes more. Whiz the soup in a liquidiser, then pass through a fine sieve into another saucepan.

When you are ready to serve, gently reheat the soup and check the seasoning to taste.

Parsley and Bacon Soup

Inspired by traditional pea and ham soup, this one has a very appealing vibrant green colour. Aim for a real blast of parsley and bacon flavours.

Serves 8

55ml (2fl oz) olive oil

3 onions, peeled and finely
  sliced

110g (4oz) parsley, stalks
  and leaves separated

850ml (1½ pints) chicken
  stock

1 medium potato, peeled
  and sliced

12 thin rashers of heavily
  smoked streaky bacon,
  chopped

50g (2oz) baby spinach

75ml (3fl oz) double cream

25g (1oz) salted butter

salt and pepper

chopped parsley and crispy
  bacon, to serve

In a large saucepan heat the olive oil. Add the onions and the parsley stalks and leave to sweat. When the onions have softened and are translucent, add the chicken stock, potato and bacon and simmer until the potato is cooked. Finally, add the parsley leaves, baby spinach and cream.

Continue to cook for a further 3 minutes, then remove from the heat and blitz in a liquidiser. Pass the soup through a fine sieve into a clean saucepan or bowl.

To serve, reheat the soup, adding the butter in small knobs, stirring continuously. Check the seasoning. I like to serve this soup with lots of chopped parsley and a strip of crispy bacon.

Prawn Bisque

Creating two dishes for the price of one is an appealing idea to anyone who runs a restaurant, which is how this recipe came into being. Having peeled a kilo of prawns one day for prawn cocktail, I decided to use the leftover shells for this wonderful, intensely flavoured prawn bisque. Of course you could just as easily turn this into a lobster bisque using lobster shells.

Serves 6

shells from 1kg (2lb 4oz)
  shell-on prawns

2 tbsp olive oil

25g (1oz) butter

1 large leek, roughly
  chopped

4 large shallots, peeled and
  roughly chopped

a squeeze of lemon juice

225g (8oz) baby vine
  tomatoes

about 725ml (1¼ pints) fish
  or chicken stock (enough to
  cover the shells)

150ml (¼ pint) whipping
  cream

40g (1½ oz) salted butter

salt and pepper

bunch of chives, snipped

Pre-heat the oven to 150C/300F/Gas 2.

Place the prawn shells in a roasting tin and put this in the pre-heated oven for about 30 minutes until the shells have dried out completely.

Meanwhile, heat the oil and butter together over a moderate heat, then sweat the chopped vegetables. Add the prawn shells, lemon juice, tomatoes and enough stock to cover. Bring slowly to the boil and simmer gently for 30 minutes.

Remove from the heat and blitz the whole lot (shells included) in a blender, before pressing the mixture through a sieve into a saucepan. Bring to the boil again and simmer to reduce by about half to intensify the flavour, skimming off any scum that appears on the surface.

When the bisque has reached the desired depth of flavour, whisk in the whipping cream followed by the butter. Just before serving, season to taste and sprinkle with snipped chives.

Velouté of Morston Mussels

I know I'm biased, but I do believe the mussels gathered at Morston are the plumpest and tastiest you can get. The only down side is that they do need a bit of work, scraping off all the barnacles. Like cockles, they are best left in the fridge overnight in a bowl of lightly salted water with plain flour scattered over (ingesting the flour encourages the mussels to spit out any sand and grit).

Serves 6

1kg (2lb 4oz) mussels,
  scraped, debearded and
  cleaned (see intro)

225ml (8fl oz) white wine

50g (2oz) butter

1 medium onion, peeled and
  finely sliced

2 level tsp plain flour

1 level tsp medium curry
  powder

150ml (¼ pint) fish or
  chicken stock

150ml (¼ pint) double cream

1 x 120g pack of baby
  spinach leaves, washed

6 tsp snipped fresh chives,
  to garnish

crusty bread, to serve

Drain the mussels in a colander then leave under cold, running water for a few minutes to get rid of the flour (see intro). Heat a large pan over a high heat until hot. Quickly throw in the mussels and the white wine. Cover and cook over a high heat, shaking the pan till all the mussels have opened. Drain them into a large colander, placed over a bowl to catch the cooking liquor.

Once the mussels are cool enough to handle, remove them from the shells and set aside in a bowl, discarding any that have not opened. Strain the cooking liquor through a muslin cloth into a bowl and reserve.

In another saucepan, melt the butter, then sweat the onion until soft. Stir in the flour and curry powder, then cook gently for a couple of minutes. Add the cooking liquor from the mussels and stock, stir well and leave to simmer for 10 minutes.

Stir in the cream, bring back to the boil and add the mussels to warm them through. Finally, just before serving, add the spinach leaves and ladle the soup into warmed bowls. Sprinkle liberally with snipped chives and serve with crusty bread.

Butter Sauce (Beurre Blanc)

To turn this into a Chive Butter Sauce for the Crab Linguine (*see* page 104) and other fish dishes, simply add 4 tbsp snipped fresh chives. Alternatively, you could use a similar amount of tarragon or parsley. It's important when adding herbs to any sauce to do so at the last minute.

Serves 6-8

2 shallots, peeled and
  finely sliced

1 tbsp white wine vinegar

2 tbsp lemon juice

4 tbsp white wine

1 tbsp cold water

225g (8oz) salted butter, cut
  into cubes

chopped fresh herbs as
  required

Place the finely sliced shallots, wine vinegar, lemon juice and white wine in a saucepan. Bring to the boil and reduce the liquid until you have about 2 tbsp. Add the cold water and reduce again until you have 1 tbsp liquid.

Turn the heat down and, over a low heat, slowly whisk in the butter, about 25g (1oz) at a time. The sauce will emulsify (thicken and lighten in colour). Once all the butter has been added, remove the pan from the heat, then pass the sauce through a sieve into another saucepan. Set aside until needed, but do not refrigerate or the sauce will separate.

To serve, gently reheat the sauce, stirring continuously. Add the chopped herbs, if using: the type of herb and quantity used will depend on what you are serving the sauce with.

Cumberland Sauce

This is the ideal traditional accompaniment to Partridge Terrine (*see* page 88), but also partners other game, ham and cold meats extremely well. I find that the easiest way to remove strips of zest from oranges and lemons is to peel them with a potato peeler, then slice the parings very thinly with a small sharp knife.

2 shallots, finely chopped

zest from 3 oranges, sliced
  into very thin strips

zest from 1 lemon, sliced
  into very thin strips

450g (1lb) redcurrant jelly

1 tbsp cider vinegar or white
  wine vinegar

1 tsp Dijon mustard

150ml (¼ pint) port

salt and pepper

Place the shallots in a small pan, cover with cold water and bring to the boil. Blanch for 1 minute then refresh immediately in cold water. Drain and set aside. Repeat this process with the strips of orange and lemon zest, blanching them for 3 minutes.

Melt the redcurrant jelly in a saucepan and stir in the cider vinegar, Dijon mustard and port. Bring this mixture to the boil, then add the shallots, orange and lemon zest. Simmer gently for about 30 minutes until reduced and slightly thickened. Finally, season the sauce with salt and pepper and serve hot or cold.

Hollandaise Sauce

Classic hollandaise sauce is delicious and has many uses, but here I have added two variations: Sauce Choron and Brown Shrimp Béarnaise. If you make hollandaise in advance, keep it in a slightly warm place, but be careful not to put it anywhere too warm, or in the fridge, or it will split.

Serves 6-8

3 egg yolks
pinch of salt
½ tsp caster sugar
1 tbsp lemon juice
1 tbsp white wine
1 tbsp white wine
  vinegar
1 shallot, peeled and
  finely sliced
12 white peppercorns,
  cracked
175g (6oz) salted butter

Place the egg yolks, salt and sugar in a food processor and give them a quick whiz. In a small pan heat the lemon juice, wine, wine vinegar, shallot and peppercorns together until the liquid has reduced by half.

Meanwhile, in another pan melt the butter and allow it to bubble but not colour. Turn on the food processor again and strain in the hot, reduced liquor, followed slowly by the hot butter.

Once all the butter has been added, pour the hollandaise sauce into a bowl and keep warm, covered with clingfilm, until needed.

Brown Shrimp Béarnaise

Brown Shrimp Béarnaise goes particularly well with skate wings and most wet fish.

1 quantity Hollandaise
  Sauce (*see* above)
110g (4oz) brown
  shrimps, peeled
2 tbsp chopped fresh
  tarragon

Make the hollandaise sauce then, just before serving, stir in the shrimps and tarragon.

Sauce Choron

The addition of tomatoes and fresh tarragon to a classic hollandaise sauce makes it the perfect accompaniment to grilled or pan-fried meat and fish dishes.

1 quantity Hollandaise Sauce
  (*see* above)
3 vine tomatoes, skinned,
  deseeded and finely diced
2 tbsp chopped tarragon

Make the hollandaise sauce then, just before serving, stir in the tomatoes and tarragon.

Lime Mayonnaise

This goes really well with cold shellfish as the lime adds a tangy element to the mayonnaise. It appears in the recipes for My Favourite Lobster Salad (*see* page 122) and Morston Hall Crab Cakes (*see* page 118) and will keep for a few days in the fridge.

Serves 8

2 limes

1 egg

1 tsp English mustard
  powder

275ml (½ pint) sunflower oil

salt and pepper

Zest 1 lime and set aside. Juice both limes and place the egg, 2 tbsp lime juice and mustard powder in the bowl of a food processor, reserving the remaining juice for later use. Season well with salt and pepper, then whiz on a high speed until all the ingredients are combined. Turn off the machine and, using a spatula, scrape down the sides of the bowl to make sure everything gets properly incorporated.

Turn the machine back on and very slowly drizzle in the sunflower oil: as you do so, the mixture will emulsify and gradually thicken. Add the grated lime zest and more juice if necessary. Check the seasoning and transfer to the fridge until needed.

Sweet-and-Sour Sauce for Fish

Although this sauce sounds Oriental, the title simply reflects the balance of sweet and sour flavourings. It works beautifully with white fish, such as turbot, sole, halibut and plaice and can be made in advance for reheating. You could also serve this with chicken, in which case use chicken stock instead of fish.

Serves 4

2 tbsp caster sugar

4 tbsp sherry wine vinegar

6 tbsp Noilly Prat

275ml (½ pint) fish stock

55ml (2fl oz) whipping cream

10g (½oz) unsalted butter

salt and pepper

Melt the sugar in a heavy-based saucepan over a low heat until it has turned a light caramel colour (do not let it burn or the sauce will be bitter).

Immediately add the vinegar, followed by the Noilly Prat. Bring to the boil and reduce by at least half, then add the stock. Continue to boil until reduced by half again. Finally, add the cream and simmer until the sauce just about coats the back of a spoon.

Just before serving, whisk in the butter over a low heat, and season with salt and pepper.

Sweet Mustard Sauce

This sauce goes well with meat dishes, particularly pork – roast ham at Christmas and Pork Fillet with Sweet Mustard Sauce and Marsala Prunes (*see* page 142). You could also serve it with gravadlax, as an alternative to the Mustard and Dill Sauce included in that recipe (*see* page 114).

Serves 4-6

3 tbsp olive oil

2 shallots or 1 medium
  onion, peeled and finely
  sliced

1 clove of garlic, peeled
  and chopped

1 carrot, peeled and finely
  sliced

1 stick of celery, sliced

1 small lobe of fresh ginger,
  peeled and crushed

150ml (¼ pint) Noilly Prat

150ml (¼ pint) chicken stock

150ml (¼ pint) whipping
  cream

2 tbsp wholegrain or Dijon
  mustard

salt and pepper

Heat the oil in a saucepan, then add the shallots and garlic. Sweat gently until softened. Add the carrot, celery, ginger and Noilly Prat and cook until the liquor has reduced by half. Add the chicken stock and reduce again by half. Finally, add the cream and bring to the boil, then simmer, reducing a little, until the sauce coats the back of a spoon.

Strain it into another pan, add the mustard, taste and season if necessary.

This sauce will keep for a few days in the fridge. To serve, simply reheat gently until warmed through.

Starters

The first course of any meal is the curtain-raiser to what should be a memorable evening, which is why it has to be a real show stopper – colourful, appealing and appetising! Guests always approach their starter with a sense of excitement, so a bit of effort pays off. The good news is that many starters can be prepared well in advance, leaving you to concentrate on the main course and avoid any last-minute hassles.

Whether at home or in the restaurant at Morston, starters are the real kick-off point for successful entertaining. One of the most rewarding parts of running the kitchen at Morston is the sense of achievement we get when we come up with a new starter, or indeed any new dish. It may simply be a variation on one of our favourite risottos or a new dressing on a salad, but you can never be quite sure it's a success until the plates come back from the dining room with everything eaten.

I might not have said this ten years ago, but some of our best starters – such as Niçoise Terrine and Roasted Red Pepper Tart – are totally meat-free. Both these dishes epitomise a great starter: packed with flavour, visually stunning and requiring no last-minute preparation beyond adding some goat's cheese or Parmesan to serve them with, if you want to. Generally, terrines make excellent starters, even if there is always that heart-stopping moment as you turn them out, hoping that they won't collapse in a heap on the plate as you cut into them!

My advice for really good vegetarian cooking is to pack every dish so full of flavour that everyone – vegetarian or not – will enjoy it (with the added bonus that the vegetarian gets to feel smug, believing that the rest of the table is beginning to see 'the light of day'!).

You can't choose a first course in isolation of the rest of the meal, however. If you choose a fish-based starter, for example, then consider a meat-based main course, or vice versa. Every meal should have a balance of flavours, textures and sauces.

So let your imagination loose and go for a dish that's really exciting and mouthwatering, yet light enough not to overwhelm your guests' appetites for what's to come.

Buttery Herbed Scrambled Eggs

This is a lovely starter or, if the occasion demands, a very special breakfast or brunch dish. At Morston we also serve it topped with smoked salmon as a fish course, and sometimes even in the eggshells, although you do have to be very careful when cracking them.

Serves 6

9 eggs

150g (5oz) butter, cut into
  small pieces

3 tbsp snipped chives

2 tbsp chopped parsley

1 tbsp chopped tarragon

1 tbsp chopped mint

salt and pepper

Break the eggs into a large bowl, beat them well and then push them through a sieve into a heavy based, non-stick saucepan. Add the pieces of butter and set aside.

Place the snipped chives, chopped parsley, tarragon and mint in a bowl.

About 20 minutes before serving, heat the eggs on the lowest possible heat, stirring continuously. Once the butter has melted, the eggs will start to cook: watch them carefully as they need to be fairly runny when served and will continue to cook after you have taken them off the heat.

Just before serving, add the herbs and check the seasoning.

Melon Sorbet with Parma Ham

This is my updated version of that old favourite, melon and Parma ham. In my long-lost youth, I went to France with some college friends to look for a summer job. As luck would have it, I ended up selling ice cream on the beach in the South of France – a good place to be in July and August, even if the sand was too hot to walk on! One day my employer caught me sitting eating melon ice cream and gave me the sack. In an effort to recreate that glorious ice cream, I've come up with this sorbet, which captures the essence of those carefree days.

Serves 6 generously

2 very ripe Charentais
  (pink-fleshed) melons

275ml (½ pint) sugar syrup
  (*see* page 214)

juice of 1 lime

6 thin slices of Parma ham

6 generous slugs of port

Scoop out the melon flesh into a liquidiser. Add about three-quarters of the sugar syrup and blitz at high speed, then taste, adding a little more syrup if needed.

Strain the mixture through a sieve into a large jug. Stir in the lime juice and taste again – it should be sweet, yet have an unmistakable melon flavour. Churn in an ice cream machine and store in a suitable container in the freezer.

To serve, place a scoop of melon sorbet on to each plate, then top with a twist of Parma ham and a slug of port.

Herb Gnocchi

This is a completely different way of cooking gnocchi but what attracts me about this recipe is that it isn't as fiddly as the small nuggets of conventional gnocchi. This recipe makes 3 rolls of gnocchi which are then tightly wrapped in clingfilm, to be sliced when cold and fried just prior to serving. The rolls can be made and stored in the fridge for three days.

Serves 4-6

3 baking potatoes, weighing about 800g (1lb 12oz) in total

40g (1½oz) plain flour, sifted, plus extra for coating the gnocchi

110g (4oz) freshly grated mature Cheddar

1 egg, plus 2 egg yolks

6 tbsp snipped chives

butter, for frying

asparagus, to serve

salt and pepper

Oven-roasted Tomato Fondue with Garlic and Thyme (*see* page 174) or salad leaves, to serve

Bake the potatoes until soft, then halve them. Scoop out the cooked flesh and push through a sieve into a large bowl.

Add the flour, Cheddar, egg, egg yolks and chives. Mix thoroughly and season to taste.

Place 3 sheets of clingfilm directly on top of each other and spoon one-third of the gnocchi mixture along the front edge about 15-20cm (6-8 inches) long, leaving plenty of room at each end. Roll the mixture up tightly in the clingfilm and tie each end tightly with string. Repeat this twice more.

Bring a pan of water to the boil, drop in the rolls of gnocchi and cook for 15 minutes. Carefully remove with a slotted spoon and refresh in a bowl of iced water. When they are cooled, remove from the water, pat dry with a clean tea towel and place in the fridge to set really well.

When you are ready to serve the gnocchi, pre-heat the oven to 180C/350F/Gas 4.

Unwrap the rolls of gnocchi, then slice them into rounds about 1cm (½ inch) thick. Toss them in a bowl of lightly seasoned flour and set aside on a plate.

Heat a frying pan over a medium heat, add a knob of butter and fry the gnocchi until coloured on both sides. Drain them on kitchen paper, transfer to a baking tray and heat through for a few minutes in the pre-heated oven.

Serve 5 or 6 discs of gnocchi per person on warmed plates with some asparagus, oven-roasted tomato fondue or salad leaves, or all three.

Herb and Parmesan Risotto with Red Wine Sauce

We have a saying in the kitchen, "You're only as good as your last risotto" and this certainly holds true, as the more you make risotto, the more adept you become at it and the better the risotto. In my first book, *Cooking at Morston Hall*, I gave a beginner's risotto. This recipe is the classical version and gives the creamiest consistency. When cooked, a risotto should be fluid (the Italians say *all'onda* – on the wave) and not stand firm.

Serves 6

For the red wine sauce

150ml (¼ pint) decent red
  wine

150ml (¼ pint) port

1 tbsp redcurrant jelly

For the risotto

1.2 litres (2 pints) chicken or
  vegetable stock

50g (2oz) salted butter

2 shallots, peeled and finely
  chopped

250g (9oz) risotto rice,
  preferably Arborio

4 tbsp white wine

50g (2oz) finely grated fresh
  Parmesan

1 tbsp finely chopped
  tarragon

3 tbsp finely chopped chives

1 tbsp finely chopped
  parsley

salt and pepper

Put the wine, port and redcurrant jelly in a saucepan and bring to a simmer, then reduce over a moderate heat until the sauce becomes quite syrupy and coats the back of a spoon (you may end up with only 65ml/2½fl oz liquid left, but this is fine as you only use a very small amount for each serving). You can make this one day ahead.

To make the risotto, heat the chicken stock over a low heat. Meanwhile, in a large saucepan, melt the butter and gently sauté the shallots. Add the rice and, stirring continuously, cook for a few minutes.

Add the white wine and cook until evaporated. Start stirring in the hot stock, a ladleful at a time, adding the next ladleful only when most of the stock has been absorbed (don't try to rush it as time is of the essence for a really successful risotto).

The risotto is ready when it is creamy in texture but not chalky, and the grains still retain some 'bite'. You may not need to use all the stock, but it's better to have it ready just in case.

Just before serving, add the Parmesan, followed by the herbs. Season to taste. Ladle the risotto into bowls, spoon around the wine sauce and serve immediately.

Mousse of Norfolk Asparagus

This very delicate mousse can be served cold or warm and the good news is that the mixture can be prepared in advance, then cooked when you are ready to serve. You don't have to serve the Parmesan Crisps (*see* page 38) with it, but I find they go particularly well with asparagus.

Serves 6

450g (1lb) Norfolk
  asparagus, plus 12-18
  extra spears to serve
  (optional)

25g (1oz) salted butter, plus
  25g (1oz) for greasing the
  ramekins

1 egg, plus 1 egg yolk

200ml (7fl oz) double cream

salt and pepper

Parmesan Crisps (*see* page
  38), to serve

6 ramekins, each 7.5cm
(3 inch) diameter

Begin by buttering the ramekins and placing them in the fridge.

Trim and discard the woody ends from the asparaus and finely chop the stems (you need 275g/10oz chopped weight).

Melt 25g (1oz) butter in a saucepan. Add the chopped asparagus and 2 tbsp water. Season lightly, cover with a lid and cook gently for about 5 minutes until the asparagus is tender.

Remove from the heat and liquidise the asparagus. With the machine still running, add the egg, egg yolk and double cream. Strain the mixture through a sieve into a jug, then pour into the cold, well-buttered ramekins.

Place the ramekins in the top of a double boiler and steam the mousses gently for about 10 minutes (they should be just set but still wobble in the centre).

To serve, run a small, sharp knife round the inside of each ramekin and turn the mousses out on to serving plates (you can also serve the mousses in the ramekins, if you prefer). Serve with a Parmesan Crisp and some extra steamed asparagus, if liked.

Muffins with Parma Ham, Poached Quails' Eggs and Hollandaise Sauce

Everything can be prepared in advance for this really delicious classic first course, which could easily be built up into a brunch dish. However, hollandaise will split if cooled and reheated, so keep it just warm in a bowl over a pan of warm water. Cracking quails' eggs can be a bit fiddly, but if you make a little slit with the point of a small knife round the middle, they are easier to crack open and you are less likely to break the yolk. Nevertheless, I still do an extra one or two, just in case.

Serves 6 as a starter

zest and juice of ½ orange

2 tbsp olive oil

½ tsp Dijon mustard

12 quails' eggs

6 muffins (*see* page 40), or
  good-quality bought ones,
  halved

softened butter, for
  spreading on the muffins

1 large bunch of watercress,
  thick stalks removed

6 thin slices of Parma or
  Bayonne ham

1 quantity of Hollandaise
  Sauce (*see* page 64)

salt and pepper

Make the dressing by mixing together the orange zest and juice, olive oil and Dijon mustard. Season with salt and pepper.

Pre-heat the grill and bring a saucepan of water to the boil.

Remove the pan of boiling water from the heat, swirl the water around, then carefully crack open the quails' eggs and drop them into the water. Leave for 1½ minutes then, using a slotted spoon, carefully remove the eggs. (This can be done 2-3 hours ahead; if so, plunge the eggs into boiling water for 30 seconds to warm them, just before serving.)

Place the halved muffins, cut side uppermost, under the grill until lightly toasted. Butter them immediately.

Lightly dress the watercress and place a small bunch on top of 6 of the halved muffins. Add a slice of ham.

Finally, place 2 quails' eggs on each watercress and ham-topped muffin. Coat with hollandaise sauce and season with salt and pepper. Serve with the remaining halved muffins.

Niçoise Terrine of Vegetables

This is a real party piece that can be made a couple of days in advance. Besides being excellent on its own, this terrine is fantastic with fish such as sea bass or cod. Don't be tempted to press the terrine too quickly; instead, place it in the fridge for at least 1 hour until about to set, before placing a weight on top. If you do it sooner you are likely to force the juice out of the top. Serve this with a slice of goat's cheese if you're feeling decadent.

Serves 10

3 red peppers

3 yellow peppers

3 orange peppers

2 cloves of garlic, peeled and
   finely grated

3 aubergines

4 courgettes

8 tbsp olive oil

2 gelatine leaves

6 vine tomatoes, skinned,
   quartered and deseeded
   (do this over a bowl,
   retaining as much juice
   as possible)

1 x 10g pack of basil leaves

salt and pepper

dressed salad leaves and
   good-quality, aged
   balsamic vinegar, to serve

a terrine mould about 25cm
long and 7.5cm deep (10 x
3 inches) lined with
clingfilm, leaving a generous
overhang

Roast the peppers with the garlic (*see* page 180) then, when cool enough to handle, remove the skins. Keep any juices and oil from the baking tray and pour them into a small pan, along with any retained tomato juice.

Heat a ridged frying pan and, while it is heating, slice the aubergines and courgettes lengthways into 5mm (¼ inch) slices. Place the courgettes and aubergines in a large bowl and coat with the olive oil. Once the frying pan is hot, place the slices of aubergine and courgettes across the ridges to colour and mark well on both sides. Set aside on separate plates.

Soak the gelatine in cold water to soften and, meanwhile, gently heat the retained juices and oil from the peppers and tomatoes in a small saucepan. Remove the gelatine, squeezing out any excess water. Add it to the warmed juices and oil and, when it has completely dissolved, take off the heat.

Line the base and the sides of the terrine with aubergine slices, leaving enough overlapping the sides to eventually fold over and cover the top. Layer the terrine with red peppers, then courgettes, lightly seasoning between each layer and adding some basil.

Spoon over some of the gelatine liquid, then continue layering with yellow peppers, tomatoes, aubergines, orange peppers and courgettes, seasoning between each layer, spooning in a little more gelatine liquid and adding as many layers of basil leaves as you like. Finally, spoon over any remaining gelatine liquid, then fold over the overlapping aubergine slices and clingfilm.

Place the terrine on a tray and put in the fridge for 1 hour. Cover with foil and place some weights on top, then return to the fridge for 2-3 hours, or preferably overnight.

To serve, carefully turn the terrine out on to a chopping board and, using a sharp, serrated knife, cut it into slices about 2.5cm (1 inch) thick. Remove the clingfilm and serve with young salad leaves lightly dressed with good-quality, aged balsamic vinegar.

Norfolk Asparagus, Sautéed New Potatoes and Crispy Bacon served with Chive Hollandaise

For six weeks, from the beginning of May, I make no excuse for having asparagus on the menu every night. This is one of our variations: if you are lucky enough to grow your own asparagus and new potatoes, it's even more sensational. Because there are several elements to this dish, it is easier if you prepare the potatoes, then the chive hollandaise and, finally, the bacon and asparagus.

Serves 6

450g (1lb) small scraped
  new potatoes

1 bunch of fresh mint

55ml (2fl oz) sunflower oil

50g (2oz) salted butter, plus
  extra for tossing the
  asparagus

6 rashers of smoked streaky
  bacon, preferably Alsace,
  very thinly sliced

3 bunches of Norfolk
  asparagus, with at least
  10 stalks in each bunch,
  trimmed

sea salt flakes and freshly
  ground black pepper

1 quantity Hollandaise Sauce
  (see page 64)

3 tbsp snipped chives

Place the new potatoes in a large saucepan, cover with cold, salted water and add the mint. Bring to the boil and cook until just tender. Drain the potatoes and allow to cool a little, then slice them into 5mm (¼ inch) slices.

Heat a frying pan over a medium heat and add the sunflower oil and butter. Once the butter is foaming, add the potatoes and fry until golden on each side (you may need to do this in two batches). Using a slotted spoon, transfer the potatoes to a baking tray and season lightly. These can be prepared ahead, then warmed through (see below).

Make the hollandaise (see page 64).

Pre-heat the oven to 180C/350F/Gas 4. Place the slices of bacon on a baking tray and cook in the oven till crisp, watching carefully. Meanwhile, on another baking tray, gently re-heat the potatoes for 10 minutes.

Bring a saucepan of salted water to a steady boil. Carefully submerge the asparagus stalks in the boiling water and cook until just tender, but still retaining some bite. Drain immediately and gently toss in a little butter.

To serve, spoon some of the re-heated sautéed potatoes on to a plate and lay about 5 stalks of asparagus on top. Season them with salt and pepper. Add the snipped chives to the hollandaise, then spoon it over the asparagus. Top each plate with a slice of crispy bacon.

Parsley Salad

This stunning, powerfully flavoured salad comes from one of our very best food writers, Simon Hopkinson, who manages to combine common sense with wit in everything he writes. Simon credits Gay Bilson for the recipe but, whatever its source, I hope you will try this. Because it's so crammed with strong flavours, you only need to serve small portions.

Serves 8 as an accompaniment

110g (4oz) flat-leaf parsley, stalks removed

50g (2oz) pitted black olives, chopped

110g (4oz) red onion, finely chopped

50g (2oz) very small capers, well rinsed

2 cloves of garlic, peeled and crushed or grated

20 anchovy fillets, preferably salted, finely chopped

zest and juice of 1 lemon

1 large red chilli, finely chopped

120ml (4fl oz) olive oil

1 ripe avocado

freshly ground black pepper

50g (2oz) Parmesan

aged balsamic vinegar (optional)

Blitz the parsley leaves as finely as possible in a food processor, then transfer them to a large bowl. Add the black olives, red onion, capers and garlic and mix thoroughly.

Add the anchovies, lemon zest and juice, chilli and olive oil. Season with freshly ground black pepper.

Just before serving, peel and finely dice the avocado. Mix it well with the other ingredients and top with freshly grated Parmesan and maybe some aged balsamic vinegar.

Partridge Terrine

I couldn't do another book without acknowledging the wonderful game we have in this country. For the last two years, I have been totally hooked on shooting, and a very good friend always brings me twelve brace of grouse on 13 August. This terrine is also really good made with grouse or pheasant if partridge is unavailable. Serve with Cumberland Sauce (*see* page 63).

Serves 10-12

6 fresh partridge, breasts
  removed and leg meat
  taken off the bone

350g (12oz) belly of pork

2 cloves of garlic, peeled

2 tbsp port

2 tbsp Marsala

2 tbsp orange juice

1 egg, beaten

1 tbsp chopped tarragon

1 tbsp chopped parsley

1 tbsp chopped mint

1 tbsp snipped chives

150ml (¼ pint) good chicken
  or game stock

250g (9oz) thinly sliced
  smoked streaky bacon

salt and pepper

Cumberland Sauce, to serve
  (*see* page 63)

30cm (12 inch) terrine mould

Take four of the partridge breasts (select any damaged ones for this) and push through a mincer together with the leg meat from all the partridges, the belly of pork and the garlic. Place in a bowl and add the port, Marsala, orange juice and a good seasoning of salt and pepper and mix well. Cover with clingfilm and place in the fridge to marinate overnight.

The next day, add the beaten egg, chopped herbs and stock, then mix thoroughly.

Pre-heat the oven to 170C/325F/Gas 3.

Line the terrine with the bacon. (Make sure there is plenty of bacon overlapping the sides, as you will use this to cover the mixture.)

Press half of the minced mixture tightly into the bottom of the lined terrine, then add the remaining 8 breasts lengthways. Cover the breasts with the remaining mixture, followed by the overlapping slices of bacon.

Place a piece of greaseproof paper over the surface of the terrine, then cover the top with foil. Put the lid on and cook in a bain marie in the pre-heated oven for 1 hour.

After an hour turn the oven temperature up to 200C/400F/Gas 6, remove the lid, foil and greaseproof paper from the top of the terrine and cook for a further 15 minutes so that the bacon colours.

Remove from the oven, cover the top of the terrine again with foil and put weights on top. Leave to cool completely and then refrigerate for at least 2 days.

Serve with Cumberland Sauce.

Peperonata

Served warm or, even better cold, this dish works particularly well with grilled fish or on its own with a rocket salad and a generous quantity of Parmesan cheese grated over. At Morston we have also been known to serve it with Buttery Herbed Scrambled Eggs (*see* page 72). A big plus point for those entertaining at home is that *peperonata* can be made a day in advance.

Serves 6

2 red peppers

2 yellow peppers

2 orange peppers

3 tbsp olive oil

2 large shallots, peeled and
finely sliced

2 cloves of garlic, peeled and
finely grated

6 vine tomatoes, skinned,
deseeded and cut into
strips

1 heaped tbsp very small
capers

2 tbsp chopped parsley

salt and pepper

Begin by roasting the peppers and removing the skins (*see* page 180).

While the peppers are roasting, heat the olive oil in a saucepan over a moderate heat, then sweat the shallots and garlic until soft. Remove from the heat and set aside.

Slice the roasted, skinned peppers fairly thinly and mix with the tomatoes and shallots. Season to taste. Just before serving, stir in the capers and chopped parsley.

Roasted Pepper Tart (Savoury Tarte Tatin)

When Neil Alston makes this at his cookery demonstrations it's a real show stopper, and it's easy to see why: the tart looks stunning, with its alternating colours of the peppers, and tastes wonderful – great if you have vegetarians to feed. I like to serve this warm with plenty of fresh Parmesan and a bowl of mixed salad leaves, but it's also delicious with roast rack of lamb.

Serves 6

4 red peppers

4 yellow peppers

4 orange peppers

olive oil and butter for frying
  the onions

3 red onions, peeled and
  sliced

25g (1oz) basil leaves

6 tomatoes, skinned,
  deseeded and halved

home-made or good-quality
  bought puff pastry

salt and pepper

20cm (8 inch) tarte Tatin tin,
sides buttered, with a circle
of good-quality greaseproof
paper lining the base.

Roast the peppers (*see* page 180).

While the peppers are roasting, add a little olive oil and butter to a hot frying pan. Turn the heat down and sauté the red onions, stirring occasionally, until softened and beginning to caramelise. Remove from the heat.

Pre-heat the oven to 200C/400F/Gas 6.

When the peppers are cool enough to handle, skin and cut into halves. Arrange half the peppers in the base of the tarte Tatin dish, skinned side downwards, pointing towards the centre and alternating red, yellow and orange slices. Sprinkle one-third of the basil leaves over the peppers. Repeat with the remaining peppers and more basil leaves, then season.

Place the tomato halves on top of the peppers, season well with salt and pepper and sprinkle with the remaining basil leaves. Finally, spread the cooked onions over the top.

Roll out the puff pastry. Cut out a circle just a little larger than the tarte Tatin tin. Place this on top of the onions, tucking in the edges. Cut little holes in the pastry, then cook in the oven for about 25 minutes, or until the pastry is golden-brown.

Remove from the oven and allow to stand for 5 minutes before turning the pepper tart out on to a large serving plate. Serve warm or cold.

Smooth Chicken Liver Pâté

We came up with this recipe as a way of using the chicken livers left over from our weekly chicken order for Morston. You won't taste a smoother pâté and, as it needs to be made at least 24 hours before serving for maximum flavour, it's a winner when entertaining at home. It's also great for a cold buffet table and can be used as a pâté to spread on beef Wellington. Quince jelly makes an interesting accompaniment as does Cumberland Sauce (*see* page 63).

Serves 12

450g (1lb) chicken livers

1 clove of garlic, grated

2 tbsp redcurrant jelly,

  melted

150ml (¼ pint) chicken

  stock, warmed

2 eggs, beaten

570ml (1 pint) double cream

pinch of freshly grated

  nutmeg

salt and pepper

25cm x 25cm x 7.5cm (10 x
10 x 3 inch) terrine mould or
loaf tin, greased with butter
and lined with good-quality
greaseproof paper.

Pre-heat the oven to 150C/300F/Gas 2.

Drain the chicken livers well and place them in the bowl of a food processor, along with the garlic and melted redcurrant jelly. Give them a good whiz then, with the machine still running, slowly pour in the warmed chicken stock.

Once the mixture is really smooth, add the beaten eggs followed by the double cream. Season with a little grated nutmeg and plenty of salt and pepper.

Pass the mixture through a fine sieve into a jug and then pour into the greased and lined terrine mould. Cover the top with greaseproof paper. Place the terrine in a bain marie in the centre of the oven and cook for about 1 hour, or until the pâté looks just set. Remove from the oven and allow to cool before placing it in the fridge until needed.

Summer Salsa

This exotic and colourful salad has become a real favourite. It started off as guacamole and, over the years, I have added mango, cucumber and roasted red peppers. Marvellously versatile, it goes well with grilled meats and fish, but is just as good eaten on its own.

Serves 6-8

2 red peppers

2 avocados, peeled and
  finely chopped

6 tbsp olive oil

juice of 2 limes, plus extra if
  needed

1 large red chilli, finely
  chopped

1 ripe mango, peeled and cut
  into small dice

1 medium red onion, peeled
  and finely chopped

3 vine tomatoes, peeled,
  deseeded and finely
  chopped

½ cucumber, peeled,
  deseeded and finely
  chopped

3 tbsp finely chopped
  coriander

2 tbsp finely chopped mint

Thai fish sauce (optional)

salt and pepper

Roast the peppers and remove the skins (*see* page 180). Chop the peppers finely or cut into fine strips and set aside.

In a large bowl, combine the avocados, olive oil, lime juice and chilli. Season, mix well, then add all the other ingredients. Check the seasoning, adding a little more lime juice if needed. (If you are not using the salsa straight away, cover the surface directly with clingfilm, then cover the top of the bowl again tightly to keep the air out and prevent any discolouring.)

When serving this salsa with fish, you could add a few drops of Thai fish sauce as a further seasoning.

CRABS
FRESH BOILED
AND DRESSED
SAMPHIRE
OYSTERS
LOBSTERS
BLAKENE
CRAB SH
OPEN

Fish

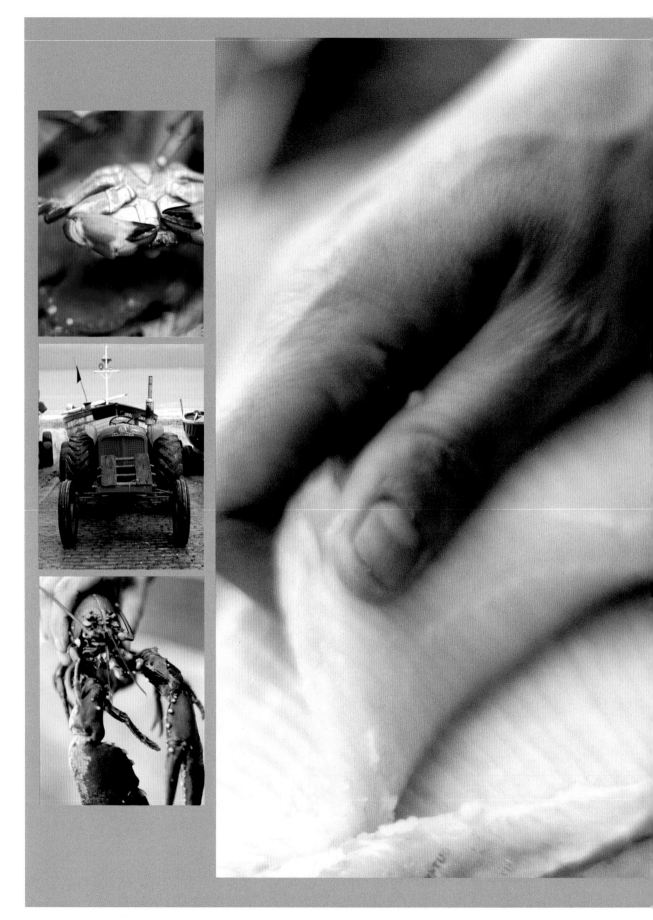

Traditionally, Friday was 'fish day' but for me every day is 'fish day'. That's because fish is a great passion of mine and, with such an abundance of wonderful wet fish caught along the North Norfolk coast and delivered to our kitchen daily, it's something we could easily take for granted.

I insist on serving fish at its best, so see no point in buying imported exotic varieties when there are myriad native species on tap. Different fish come into their own at different times: skate, for example, is at its best in January, February and March, as are herring, codling and mussels. As the seasons change, we go for lobsters, crab, plaice, turbot, halibut and wild sea bass.

Since we've been at Morston, Tracy and I have noticed enormous changes in the local catch. Fifteen years ago, sea bass was only caught from May to September, then they would leave for warmer waters. These days, however, we still get decent-sized beach-caught bass – up to 10lb in weight – in January. Cod caught at Weybourne, Salthouse or Cley invariably weighed in at over 5lb, but stocks have so diminished that we rarely see a cod over 3lb.

I am lucky enough to have a unique relationship with John Griffin, who runs the North Norfolk Fish Company in Holt. He phones me first thing every morning to run through his haul and offer advice on that evening's menu, influencing me hugely as to what we decide to cook.

When cooking fish my motto is always to 'keep it fresh and keep it simple'. If you are lucky enough to buy wonderfully fresh, locally caught fish don't drown it with heavy sauces. The freshest fish, simply and quickly grilled, baked or fried and served with a light butter sauce, cannot be bettered. And even though bought fish and chips can be good, it's simplicity itself to crumb some plaice. Get the children to help, as it will encourage them into the kitchen, something I'm all in favour of.

I am fully aware that some people still shy away from eating fish – even my older and wiser brother, Andrew, only grudgingly eats it, probably due to memories of fish at school that was less than fresh and smelt and tasted very fishy (I maintain that really fresh fish doesn't smell or taste 'fishy' at all.)

Fortunately, anti-fish feeling hasn't taken hold in the next generation. On a sleepover with schoolfriends, our son Harry was taken to the local chippie and asked what he'd like, to which he replied, "Sea bass and chips please!" And in the summer we often pile into our crab boat and tumble out at the watch house at Blakeney Point for an unforgettable picnic of fresh lobster and crab, with plenty of white wine.

If convenience food is defined as 'quick and easy' then fish must surely be the perfect convenience food – minimal preparation and easy to cook.

Char-grilled Smoked Salmon with Guacamole

This recipe offers even the most inexperienced cook something easy and different to do with smoked salmon. As always, buy the best smoked salmon you can and have the steaks cut from the centre, at least 1cm (½ inch) thick so that you can get char-grilled lines on both sides of the fish and still leave the centre fairly rare.

Serves 6

For the guacamole

2 ripe avocados

75ml (3fl oz) olive oil

juice of 2 limes

3 tomatoes, skinned,
deseeded and finely diced

2 cloves of garlic, peeled and
finely chopped

2 shallots, peeled and
chopped

1 red chilli, deseeded and
very finely chopped

2 tbsp chopped fresh
coriander

salt and pepper

For the salmon

450g (1lb) smoked salmon,
cut into 1-2cm (½-¾ inch)
thick steaks

lightly dressed salad leaves,
to serve

Make the guacamole. Cut the avocados in half, then take out the stones. Remove the skin and cut the flesh into chunky dice. Place this in a bowl with all the other ingredients, mix well and season. Cover the surface tightly with a layer of clingfilm, then cover the bowl with another layer of clingfilm and set aside.

To char-grill the salmon, heat a heavy-based ridged frying pan until it is nearly smoking. Place the salmon steaks across the ridges of the pan and press down for no longer than 30 seconds. Turn the steaks over and repeat on the other side.

Serve the salmon immediately with the guacamole and some lightly dressed salad leaves.

Crab Linguine

This exciting recipe takes Norfolk crab to new heights! Although it involves some work, the end result is so bursting with flavour that I promise you it's worth it. To make things easier, the crab meat, cream mixture and chive butter sauce can all be prepared in advance. I get my crab and lobster from Willie Weston in Blakeney, who started his business in his back room and now has several outlets – a great example of local enterprise. You may also like to try your hand at catching your own crabs: we've spent many a happy afternoon sitting on the quay, crab lines baited with chunks of bacon. The Blackiston family record is 130 crabs in one afternoon but, sadly, they are not the edible type.

Serves 6

1 quantity Chive Butter
  Sauce (*see* page 62)

4 decent-sized dressed
  crabs

75ml (3fl oz) white wine

2 tsp lemon juice

150ml (¼ pint) double cream

500g (1lb 2oz) fresh or dried
  linguine

a splash of olive oil

a knob of butter

4 tbsp chopped coriander

1 mild red chilli, finely
  chopped

salt and pepper

Make the Chive Butter Sauce (omitting the chives) and set aside.

Separate the crab meat: using your fingers, carefully flake the white meat, removing any bits of shell, then season. Place the dark meat in a food processor, season, and process on a high speed. Put the white and dark crab meat into separate bowls, cover with clingfilm and place in the fridge until needed.

Pour the white wine and lemon juice into a heavy-based saucepan and, over a high heat, reduce by half. Add the double cream, season then reduce a little more. Remove from the heat and set aside.

Cook the pasta in a large pan of rapidly boiling salted water with a splash of olive oil added. (Fresh linguine will take just a few minutes; if using dried pasta, follow the packet instructions.) While it is cooking, dip a fork in to taste it: the pasta should retain a little 'bite'. Remove from the heat and drain thoroughly. Refresh under cold water to remove the starch, then return to the pan.

Gently reheat the cream mixture, then stir in a knob of butter and the chopped coriander. Pour this on to the cooked pasta. Over a very low heat, mix gently but thoroughly. Finally, stir in the seasoned white crab meat together with the chopped chilli and mix well. Gently reheat the Chive Butter Sauce and add the snipped chives.

To serve, spoon chive butter sauce into the centre of each pasta bowl. Wrap some linguine around a fork and place on top of the sauce. Using two teaspoons, make a small quenelle of dark crab meat and sit it on top of the linguine (you will have a lot of dark crab meat left over: you could use it as a sauce in another pasta recipe). Serve immediately.

Crab Tart

I make no excuses for including three crab recipes in this book, as crab and lobster play such an important part in our menu-planning from May to October. Like most home cooks, I nearly always buy ready-dressed crabs; my supplier always sells me what he describes as 'full' crabs: ones that are packed full of meat. This tart really smacks of crab and is better eaten warm rather than piping hot to allow all the flavour to come through. To save time, both the pastry case and the custard can be prepared ahead. You can either buy dressed crabs for this recipe, separate the white and dark meat and spread the dark meat on the base of the pastry case or, if you prefer, just buy white crab meat to stir into the custard.

Serves 6

1 x 23cm (9 inch) flan ring,
4cm (1½ inches) deep, lined
with savoury shortcrust
pastry (*see* page 24)

For the custard

3 eggs, plus 2 egg yolks
425ml (¾ pint) whipping
  cream
pinch of freshly grated
  nutmeg

For the crab filling

3 dressed crabs or 450g
  (1lb) white crab meat
2 tbsp olive oil
2 bunches of spring onions,
  finely sliced
40g (1½ oz) freshly grated
  Parmesan cheese
salt and pepper
lightly dressed salad leaves
  and new potatoes, to serve
  (optional)

Pre-heat the oven to 180C/350F/Gas 4.

Cover the pastry-lined flan ring with baking parchment, fill with baking beans and place in the centre of the pre-heated oven. Bake 'blind' for about 30 minutes, or until the pastry just starts to colour.

Carefully remove the baking beans and parchment: if there are any cracks in the pastry, use leftover pieces of pastry or beaten egg to fill them. Return the pastry case to the oven for about 5 minutes. Leave to cool.

Make the custard. Place the eggs, egg yolks and double cream in a bowl and beat gently, adding nutmeg, salt and pepper. Pass through a sieve into a pouring jug. (This could be done in advance.)

If using dressed crabs, separate the crab meat with your fingers, removing any bits of shell and flaking the white meat. Spread the dark crab meat over the base of the pastry case.

Heat the olive oil in a frying pan, then quickly fry the spring onions until just softened. Add them to the pastry case. Stir the white crab meat and the Parmesan into the custard mixture, lightly season and then carefully pour it on to the spring onions.

Place the tart on a baking tray in the centre of the pre-heated oven. Cook for about 50 minutes, or until the filling is just set. Leave to cool for a few minutes before serving with some lightly dressed salad leaves and new potatoes.

Easy Smoked Salmon with Horseradish Cream

So easy that it's perfect for entertaining or at Christmas, when you don't want last-minute hassles – as long as you follow two rules. First, you must buy the very best-quality smoked salmon you can find (we get wonderful wild Irish smoked salmon from John Griffin at the North Norfolk Fish Company in Holt). The second rule is to slice it wafer-thin.

Serves 6

450g (1lb) unsliced smoked

   salmon

50g (2oz) shallot, peeled and

   finely chopped

25g (1oz) very small capers

   (or larger capers, chopped)

25g (1oz) gherkins, finely

   chopped

2 hard-boiled eggs, finely

   grated

25g (1oz) finely chopped

   flat-leaf parsley

1 lime, cut into 6 wedges

For the horseradish
cream

50g (2oz) horseradish sauce

150ml (¼ pint) crème fraîche

juice of ½ lemon

cayenne pepper

freshly ground black pepper

Place some smoked salmon on to each plate and grind a little black pepper over. Scatter the shallot, capers, gherkins, egg and parsley generously around the salmon.

Make the horseradish cream. In a bowl, mix the horseradish sauce with the crème fraîche and lemon juice. Place a teaspoonful of the horseradish cream in the centre of each serving of smoked salmon, adding a pinch of cayenne to each one. Serve with lime wedges.

Fillet of Plaice with Crumbs and Tartare Sauce

This is fish as it should be – cooked very simply, allowing its freshness to shine through. I tend to use brioche for the breadcrumbs, as it gives a very fine crumb and we always seem to have some left over in the kitchen.

Serves 6

For the tartare sauce

1 egg

1 tbsp lemon juice

1 tbsp white wine vinegar

¼ tsp sugar

¼ tsp English mustard
  powder

275ml (½ pint) sunflower oil

1 large shallot, peeled and
  very finely chopped

6 small cornichons or
  gherkins, finely diced

10g (½oz) very small capers

2 tbsp chopped flat-leaf
  parsley

1 tbsp chopped tarragon

1 tbsp snipped chives

sea salt flakes and coarsely
  ground black pepper

For the plaice

6 even-sized plaice fillets,
  skinned

75g (3oz) seasoned plain
  flour

175g (6oz) very fine
  breadcrumbs

2 eggs and 150ml (¼ pint)
  milk, beaten together to
  make an egg wash

a little butter and oil, for
  frying

salad leaves, to serve

For the tartare sauce, place the egg, lemon juice, vinegar, sugar and mustard powder in a food processor, Season with sea salt flakes and coarsely ground black pepper. Whiz on high speed for a few seconds then, using a spatula, scrape down the sides of the bowl. Turn the machine on again at high speed and, very slowly, add the sunflower oil in a steady stream until it has thickened and emulsified.

Transfer the mayonnaise to a bowl and carefully fold in the remaining ingredients. Check the seasoning.

Pre-heat the oven to 200C/400F/Gas 6.

Trim the plaice fillets and cut in half lengthways. Put the seasoned flour and breadcrumbs on to separate plates and the egg wash in a shallow bowl. Dip the first plaice fillet into the flour, shaking off any excess.

Next, dip the flour-coated fillet into the egg wash before finally dipping it into the breadcrumbs, making sure it is properly coated. Place on a baking tray and repeat with the other fillets. (You could prepare the recipe to this stage up to 8 hours before serving.)

Heat a large frying pan over a medium heat. When it is hot, add a splash of oil followed by a knob of butter. Once the butter is foaming, quickly add the plaice fillets, season and fry on both sides till lightly coloured (it may be necessary to do this in two batches to avoid overcrowding the pan). If the plaice fillets are thin, pan-fry them until cooked; alternatively, thicker fillets can be transferred to a baking tray and finished in the pre-heated oven, giving them an extra 4-5 minutes.

Serve with the tartare sauce and simply dressed salad leaves.

Gravadlax of Salmon with Mustard and Dill Sauce

Available in many guises, each gravadlax recipe varies in the amount of salt and sugar used in its preparation. The quantities given here make it easier to prepare at home and you can really taste the citrus flavours and the mustard. It's also a great recipe for entertaining as it has to be made at least three days ahead of serving.

Serves at least 8

900g (2lb) side of fresh
  salmon, pin bones removed
  and skin left on
60g (2½oz) sea salt flakes
40g (1½oz) light brown soft
  sugar
1 tbsp coriander seeds,
  crushed
1 tsp white peppercorns,
  crushed
2 large bunches of fresh dill
grated zest and juice of
  1 orange
grated zest and juice of
  1 lemon
4 tbsp Dijon mustard
Mustard and Dill Sauce (*see*
  below), and thinly sliced
  brown bread, to serve

Make the marinade. Place the sea salt, sugar, coriander seeds, peppercorns, 1 bunch of chopped dill, orange and lemon zest in a large bowl. Mix thoroughly.

Spread half the marinade on to a large baking tray. Lay the salmon on top, skin side down, and cover with the remaining marinade.

Cover with clingfilm and refrigerate for 24 hours, turning it at least once, by which time most of the salt and sugar will have become liquid.

The next day, lift the salmon out of the marinade (retaining the liquid) and wash it to remove the salt. Chop the remaining dill, then combine with the orange and lemon juice and mustard in a bowl. Return the salmon to the marinade, skin side down, then brush this mixture liberally all over the salmon. Cover again with clingfilm and refrigerate for a further 48 hours, spooning the mustard and lemon mixture over the fish daily.

Slice the salmon as thinly as possible with a very sharp knife and arrange on a serving plate. Serve with Mustard and Dill sauce and thinly sliced brown bread.

Mustard and Dill Sauce

6 tbsp homemade or good-
  quality bought mayonnaise
grated zest and juice of
  1 lime
1 tbsp black treacle
1 tbsp grain mustard
  (Pommery)
3 tbsp chopped dill
salt and pepper

Combine all the ingredients in a bowl, stir well and season if necessary.

Serve as an accompaniment to gravadlax.

Grilled Sea Bass with Purple Sprouting Broccoli and Parmentier Potatoes

From May until late autumn, stunning sea bass is caught off our coast – I've even caught some myself! Occasionally I receive a late-night phone call or a tap on the kitchen door and there on the doorstep is the freshest sea bass you could wish for. Such a wonderful fish needs little attention, and you can't get much simpler than this. You could always use asparagus or, for that matter, any young green vegetable, instead of broccoli.

Serves 4

1 large sea bass, weighing
   at least 1kg (2lb 4oz)
1 tbsp olive oil
salt and pepper
buttered purple sprouting
   broccoli (*see* page 172) and
   parmentier potatoes and
   celeriac (*see* page 164), to
   serve

Ask your fishmonger to scale and fillet the bass, then remove the pin bones. Lightly score the skin with a sharp knife and cut each fillet in half to give 4 portions.

Pre-heat the grill 10 minutes before serving.

Brush the sea bass fillets with oil, season on the flesh side and place them, skin side up, on a grill pan or baking tray. Cook under the hottest part of the grill for about 5 minutes, depending on the thickness of the fish, until the skin blackens (if the flesh just starts to come away from the skin when you turn it over, the bass is cooked).

Serve with buttered purple sprouting broccoli and parmentier potatoes.

Morston Hall Crab Cakes with Lime Mayonnaise

For busy cooks, the good news is that these crisp-crusted crab cakes can be prepared in advance and then pan-fried or deep-fried five minutes before serving. Lime Mayonnaise (*see* page 66) makes the perfect accompaniment. Instead of serving the dark crab meat as a garnish, you could use it to make smaller crab cakes, or combine it with the white crab meat in this recipe.

Serves 8

8 dressed crabs

2 egg yolks, beaten

4 tbsp chopped coriander

seasoned plain flour, for
   coating

1 egg, beaten with 75ml
   (3fl oz) milk

175g (6oz) white
   breadcrumbs

a splash of sunflower oil

juice of ½ lime

1 tsp anchovy essence

1 tbsp crème fraîche

a splash of olive oil

a knob of butter

salt and pepper

Using your fingers, separate the crab meat, removing any bits of shell and flaking the white meat. In a bowl, combine the white crab meat with the beaten egg yolks and the coriander. Season to taste.

Divide the mixture into 8 and, using your hands, form 8 even-sized crab cakes. Place them on a tray and freeze for 30 minutes to firm the mixture up. Meanwhile, put the seasoned flour, egg wash and breadcrumbs into separate bowls.

Remove the crab cakes from the freezer. Dip each crab cake into the seasoned flour to cover, then into the egg wash, shaking off any excess flour and egg wash as you go. Finally, dip each one into the breadcrumbs, making sure they are lightly and evenly coated. Place the finished crab cakes on a tray lined with greaseproof paper, cover with clingfilm and keep in the fridge until needed.

Place the dark crab meat, a splash of sunflower oil, the lime juice, anchovy essence and crème fraîche in a food processor and whiz on high speed until smooth, then taste and season. Transfer to a bowl and refrigerate until needed.

To cook the crab cakes, heat a large, heavy-based frying pan over a medium heat and, once hot, add a splash of olive oil together with a knob of butter. Fry the crab cakes gently for about 4 minutes on each side until they are golden.

Serve with Lime Mayonnaise and a small scoop of the brown crab meat mixture on the side.

Morston Prawn Cocktail

Always try to buy shell-on prawns from the cold North Atlantic or Greenland waters as they have been frozen within minutes of being caught, giving a much better flavour than you will find with shelled prawns. Shelling prawns is well worth the time and effort and, of course, you can use the shells to make a really good bisque (*see* page 58)!

Serves 6

900g (2lb) shell-on prawns

2 ripe avocados

juice of 2 limes

1 shallot, peeled and finely chopped

2 vine tomatoes, peeled, deseeded and chopped

2 tbsp chopped fresh coriander

6 tbsp olive oil

2 Little Gem lettuces, shredded

½ cucumber, peeled and diced

salt and pepper

paprika, to serve

For the Marie Rose sauce

6 tbsp home-made mayonnaise (or really good-quality bought mayonnaise)

2 tbsp tomato ketchup

1 tsp Worcestershire sauce

a splash of Cognac

a squeeze of lime juice

sea salt flakes

Peel the prawns and set aside. Peel the avocados, chop into small dice and place in a bowl. Add the lime juice, shallot, tomatoes and coriander, then taste and adjust the seasoning. Add the olive oil and mix well. Place a sheet of clingfilm directly over the avocado mixture and another sheet over the bowl – this will keep the air out and stop it from discolouring.

Make the Marie Rose sauce by combining all the ingredients in a bowl. Taste and adjust the seasoning, then cover and store in the fridge.

When you are ready to assemble the dish, arrange the lettuce and cucumber in the bottom of 6 suitable serving glasses. Top with avocado mixture, then a generous number of prawns. Spoon over the Marie Rose sauce and finish with a pinch of paprika before serving.

My favourite Lobster Salad with Mango Salsa

Definitely one of my desert island dishes – simple and full of flavour. Just 12 hours after the lobster men leave from Morston quay to set the pots, we can have their catch on the menu – you can't get fresher than that! I have fairly strong views about the size of lobsters: no more than 700g (1½lb) or they can be tough. One rather cheffy tip when opening a lobster is to look for the green, gungy jelly. As it cooks, it turns the most wonderful coral colour and is much loved by chefs for colouring and flavouring sauces.

Serves 6

3 cooked lobsters, each
  700g (1½lb), or 6 cooked
  lobsters if you want to
  serve this as a main course

For the mango salsa

1 very ripe mango, peeled
  and diced
1 medium red onion, peeled
  and finely chopped
2 ripe avocados, peeled and
  diced
1 large red chilli, deseeded
  and finely chopped
½ cucumber, peeled,
  deseeded and finely
  chopped
150ml (¼ pint) sunflower oil
juice of 2 limes
4 tbsp freshly chopped
  coriander
salt and pepper

To serve

a few small new potatoes,
  boiled; lightly dressed
  salad leaves (optional);
  home-made Lime
  Mayonnaise (*see* page 66)

Mix the mango salsa ingredients together in a bowl. Check the seasoning, then place a piece of clingfilm tightly over the surface of the salsa, followed by another piece over the bowl so that it doesn't discolour. Place in the fridge up to 1 day in advance.

Place the lobsters on a chopping board. Twist off the heads and snap off the large claws, then set aside. Using a pair of kitchen shears, cut along the back of the lobster and break the shell off the meat.

Break the claws apart and bash them open with a rolling pin or small hammer. Then, using a pointed knife, remove all the meat from the claws, trying to keep it as whole as possible. (You can use the lobster head, shells and claws for lobster bisque: see Prawn Bisque recipe on page 58.)

To serve, place some mango salsa and a few small new potatoes on each plate, plus some lightly dressed salad leaves (optional). Top each serving with a portion of lobster, making sure there is an equal amount of meat from the claws and body. Finally, serve with a dollop of home-made Lime Mayonnaise (*see* page 66) and samphire, if in season.

Roasted Halibut Steaks with Leeks and Gruyère

Ask your fishmonger to cut the steaks from the middle of the fish, preferably a large one weighing at least 4.5kg (10lb), so that they are of equal thickness and will cook evenly. If you are using halibut off the bone, it will need less cooking time.

Serves 6

24 baby leeks or spring
   onions, trimmed, topped
   and tailed

25g (1oz) salted butter

25ml (1fl oz) olive oil

6 halibut steaks on the bone,
   each weighing about 175g
   (6oz)

110g (4oz) Gruyère cheese,
   finely grated

salt and pepper

Oven-roasted Tomato Fondue
   with Garlic and Thyme (see
   page 174), to serve
   (optional)

Pre-heat the oven to 200C/400F/Gas 6.

Cook the baby leeks in a pan of boiling, salted water until just tender but still retaining their shape and colour. Drain well, refresh under cold, running water, drain again and return to the pan. Add half the butter and season with salt and freshly ground black pepper. Set aside, covered with clingfilm.

Heat a non-stick frying pan, then add the oil followed by the remaining butter. Once it is foaming, fry the halibut steaks on each side until lightly golden (you may need to do this in batches to avoid overcrowding the pan). Remove the steaks and place on a trivet in a roasting tin. Roast in the pre-heated oven for 8-10 minutes, until they are just cooked.

Meanwhile, carefully re-heat the leeks on a medium heat.

To serve, arrange some leeks neatly on each serving plate and place the fish on top. Sprinkle a generous amount of Gruyère over each steak, allowing the heat from the fish to melt the cheese (alternatively, return the steaks briefly to the oven). If you are feeling really indulgent you could serve this with Oven-roasted Tomato Fondue with Garlic and Thyme (see page 174), which would need to be made well in advance.

Scallops baked in the Shell with Puff Pastry

For a real taste of the sea, you need hand-dived scallops in their shells, as long as you're adept at shucking and cleaning them. If you're not, you could buy loose scallops and bake them in greaseproof paper. This dish can be prepared well in advance; the scallops will be cooked in the time it takes to cook the puff pastry so it is really important to roll the pastry out as thinly as you can, otherwise it will take too long to cook and the scallops will be overdone.

Serves 6

175g (6oz) home-made or
  good-quality bought puff
  pastry

2 egg yolks

12 scallops in their shells

6 tsp olive oil

2 shallots, finely chopped

1 lobe of fresh ginger, peeled
  and grated

6 tsp snipped chives

salt and pepper

Butter Sauce (Beurre Blanc,
  see page 62), to serve

crusty bread, to serve

Roll out the puff pastry as thinly as possible into a 30 x 25cm (12 x 10 inch) rectangle. Place the pastry on a chopping board and brush with egg wash made from the egg yolks mixed with a little water. Keep in the fridge until needed.

Shuck the scallops (retaining the shells) and remove the skirt. Gently wash the scallops and coral, then place on a clean tea towel and set aside. Wash the shells thoroughly in hot soapy water, rinse and dry well.

Next, place 2 of the scallops, with their corals, into the curved half of one of the shells. Pour over 1 teaspoon olive oil, then add a good pinch of the shallot, a little grated ginger and 1 teaspoon chives. Season lightly and place the flat lid of the shell on top.

Take the pastry out of the fridge and cut a strip lengthways about 2.5cm (1 inch) wide. Making sure you place it egg wash side against the scallop shell, use it to seal the two halves of the shell together. Repeat this process until all 6 shells are filled and sealed. (This could be done in the morning and the sealed shells kept in the fridge until you are ready to serve them.)

Twenty minutes before serving, pre-heat the oven to 200C/400F/Gas 6.

Remove the scallops in their shells from the fridge and brush the pastry again with egg wash. Place the shells on a baking tray and cook for about 8 minutes, until the pastry is golden.

Serve the scallops in their shells, with a separate dish of butter sauce and some crusty bread.

Skate with Beurre Noisette

Our wonderful fish man brings me skate wings so brimming with freshness they're still slimy. This is crucial with skate – if less than fresh, it smells of ammonia and should be avoided at all costs. I prefer to use large skate wings, taken off the bone so that I can gauge more accurately when the fish is cooked. This is an easy process, but if you'd rather cook the fish on the bone, it will just take a little longer. You can make the beurre noisette in advance; if doing so, remember not to add the capers and parsley until the last moment.

Serves 4

2 tbsp olive oil

25g (1oz) butter

4 skate wings, taken off the
  bone and skinned

salt and pepper

new potatoes, to serve

For the beurre noisette

110g (4oz) salted butter

juice of 1 large lemon

2 tbsp very small capers

3 tbsp chopped parsley

Pre-heat the oven to 200C/400F/Gas 6.

While the oven is heating, make the beurre noisette: melt the butter in a saucepan over a medium heat, then continue cooking until it starts to turn golden. (You are aiming for caramel-coloured granules in the butter.) Add the lemon juice and boil for 2 minutes. Set aside.

Heat a frying pan until hot, then add the oil and butter. Once the butter is foaming, add the skate wings and fry until coloured on both sides (really fresh wings may start to shrink and curl but this is normal).

Remove the skate wings from the frying pan and place on a baking tray with thick pieces together on one tray, thin on the other, for even cooking results. Season with salt and pepper and place in the oven for about 5 minutes, depending on how thick the wings are (the fish should just start to come apart when pressed).

To serve, warm the beurre noisette, add the capers and parsley and spoon it over each skate wing, making sure each person has plenty of capers. Serve with new potatoes.

Taramasalata

Although the bright pink fish paste sold in supermarkets as taramasalata may be rather tasty as a dip, it's nothing like the real thing. If you can get a whole smoked cod's roe and make it yourself you won't have that lurid pink colour, but what you will have is a wonderful summery dip or starter that's lovely with home-made bread and a salad. One word of warning: don't be tempted to use strong olive oil as it fights with the cod's roe and can result in a rather unpalatable 'goo.'

Serves 6

350g (12oz) lightly smoked

  soft cod's roe

juice of 3 lemons

2-3 cloves of garlic

  (depending on how garlicky

  you want it), peeled and

  crushed

4 tbsp fresh breadcrumbs

200ml (7fl oz) sunflower oil

200ml (7fl oz) olive oil

salt and pepper

warm crusty bread, to serve

Halve the cod's roe, scrape it away from the skin and place it in the bowl of a food processor. Add the lemon juice, crushed garlic and breadcrumbs, then give it a good whiz on high speed.

Mix the oils together in a jug. Then, with the motor still running, add the oil very slowly in a steady stream as you would for mayonnaise until the mixture has a dropping consistency – if it gets too thick add a splash of hot water to loosen it.

Scrape the tarasamalata into a bowl, taste and season if necessary. Serve with crusty bread.

Warm Lemon Sole and Smoked Salmon Mousse

Updated here for the 21st century, this luxurious dish was a regular on the menu when I cooked at John Tovey's Miller Howe Hotel in the Lake District. It can be prepared in advance and cooked at the last minute, making it a great choice for entertaining.

Serves 8

175g (6oz) smoked salmon, diced

150ml (¼ pint) milk

softened butter for brushing the ramekins twice

225g (8oz) skinned lemon sole

2 eggs

110g (4oz) thinly sliced smoked salmon, for lining the ramekins

425ml (¾ pint) double cream

salt and pepper

Hollandaise Sauce, to serve (*see* page 64)

8 ramekins, each 7.5cm (3 inches) in diameter

Cover the diced smoked salmon with the milk to remove some of the salt and oil from the fish; leave for 6-8 hours. Butter the ramekins well with softened butter and place in the fridge. When cool, brush with butter again and return to the fridge.

Dice the lemon sole. Process it in a food processor on high speed, add 1 of the eggs and give it a good whiz until thoroughly mixed. Scrape the mixture into a large bowl and season well with salt and pepper. (At Morston, we pass the processed mixture through a fine sieve or *tamis* which you could do at home for the smoothest possible texture – but, I warn you, this is quite a task.)

Strain the milk from the diced salmon, pat it dry with kitchen paper, then repeat the process as for the lemon sole, seasoning with freshly ground black pepper. Cover both bowls with clingfilm and set aside to chill in the fridge, preferably overnight.

Pre-heat the oven to 180C/350F/Gas 4.

Line the inside of each ramekin with a strip of smoked salmon.

Take the sole mixture from the fridge and, using a spatula, slowly beat in about 225ml (8fl oz) double cream a little at a time (or enough to achieve a firm consistency). Repeat this procedure with the salmon mixture.

Spoon the sole mixture into a piping bag with a 1cm (½ inch) plain nozzle. Carefully pipe about an eighth of the mixture round the inside of each ramekin, leaving a space in the centre if possible. Repeat this process for all the ramekins.

Next, fill the same piping bag with the salmon mixture. Push the nozzle through to the base of the ramekin and pipe about an eighth of the salmon mixture into each ramekin.

Put the filled ramekins in a bain marie on the centre shelf of the oven and cook for 20-25 minutes until the mousses are slightly risen and barely golden on top.

Serve the mousses warm in the ramekins or, using a sharp knife, turn out on to plates. Serve accompanied with some home-made Hollandaise Sauce (*see* page 64).

Meats

When buying meat, one of the most important things to know is its provenance. Sourcing food may be a highly fashionable subject at the moment, but I'm not jumping on any foodie bandwagon here: for me it's always been important to know where my meat has come from. And the only way to do this is to build up a good working relationship with a quality butcher.

Most of our meat comes from Arthur Howell, who has shops at Wells, Burnham Market and Binham, as well as his own abattoir. He and I both know where the meat has come from and how long it has been hung for, thus ensuring that only the very best meat, in prime condition, arrives in the kitchen at Morston. My love of shooting has also allowed me to bag my own birds, drawing on Norfolk's wonderful pheasant and partridge.

Really good, quality meat that has been well hung needs little complicated cooking and only very simple accompaniments, but there are several golden rules: seal meat well all over in a hot pan over a high heat (this can be done in advance); place it on a trivet in the roasting tin, so heat circulates all round the meat, giving more even cooking results, and allow enough time for the meat to 'rest' in a warm place after cooking and before carving.

Prime cuts, by their nature, will result in tender meat when cooked. But a return to real cooking means things like stews, braised dishes and steak and kidney pudding. These slow-cooked dishes use more muscular cuts of meat, which need longer cooking time – and more skill on the part of the cook – if they are to break down into something succulent. Your patience will be rewarded with meat that's extremely tender, plus a much deeper and more intense flavour – just think about the satisfaction in eating a really good stew, or a meltingly tender shoulder of lamb, their sauces mopped up with creamy mashed potatoes. Think, too, of the joy of cutting into a proper steak and kidney pudding and watching all those wonderful juices start to ooze out. Simple things done really well: that's what interests me.

My return to real cooking has also meant a sea change in the way I cook meat. Like most chefs, I used to add elaborate sauces, which often masked the meat's true flavour and quality and gave the sauce the starring role. These days, as in so many other things, I prefer to let the main ingredient take centre stage – the sauces and accompaniments are there to enhance, not overpower. This means keeping recipes simple and using cuts in the traditional way, bearing in mind that you need to match the meat with the correct cooking method, which is again where your butcher can prove invaluable.

Meat also brings seasonal highlights: mouthwatering spring lamb, prime beef, fed on summer pastures, flavourful autumn lamb, the first game birds of the season. Concentrate on source, quality and seasonality and, as with so much in the world of ingredients, you won't go wrong.

Braised Shoulder of Lamb with Gravy and Apple Sauce

Apple sauce with lamb may seem a little unusual, but it works really well in this recipe. This dish benefits from really slow cooking so that the meat is tender and melts in the mouth. Ask your butcher to take the shoulder off the bone and remove as much fat as possible before tying it up tightly. There will be quite a lot of delicious stock left over after the lamb has been cooked; this can always be frozen and used for other dishes. Mashed Parsley Potatoes (*see* page 176) would be my vegetable of choice with this lamb dish and are great for mopping up the gravy.

Serves 6

about 25ml (1fl oz) olive oil

about 25g (1oz) butter

2.25kg (5lb) shoulder of lamb, boned and rolled

1 large onion, peeled and chopped

1 carrot, peeled and chopped

2 sticks of celery, chopped

1 leek, sliced

3 cloves of garlic, peeled and sliced

1 sprig of rosemary

about 1.75 litres (3 pints) chicken stock, or enough to cover the lamb

1 large Bramley apple

50g (2oz) granulated sugar

salt and pepper

Pre-heat the oven to 140C/275F/Gas 1.

Heat a frying pan over a high heat, then add the olive oil followed by the butter. Add the lamb, turning to seal and colour all over.

Transfer the lamb to a deep saucepan, then add the root vegetables, garlic and rosemary. Season and add enough stock to cover.

Bring up to a simmer on top of the stove, removing any scum that appears, then cover with a lid or foil. Cook in the oven for a minimum of 4 hours, by which time the meat will be extremely tender.

Meanwhile, make the apple sauce. Peel, core and slice the apple, place it in a saucepan and cover with the sugar. Add a generous splash of water and cook over a moderate heat until very soft and pulpy. Set aside.

Once the lamb has been cooking for 3 hours, make the gravy. Remove about 1 litre (1¾ pints) stock and, in another pan, bring it to the boil. Simmer until it has reduced by half or even more, tasting until the flavour has intensified. Set aside.

When the lamb is ready, gently reheat the gravy and apple sauce. Place the lamb on a carving board and cut into chunky slices with a really sharp knife. Place a few slices on each plate, pour some gravy over and add a little blob of apple sauce to serve.

Daube of Beef

Year after year at my demonstrations at Morston I have been asked to show a really good stew and, in my opinion, the very best stew is this one, made with beef skirt – you may need to order this from your butcher several days in advance. As with most stews, it is better eaten the day after it is made.

Serves 4 generously

25g (1oz) dripping or 3 tbsp
  vegetable oil

about 900g (2lb) beef skirt

2 medium onions, peeled
  and sliced

2 large carrots, peeled and
  diced

2 sticks of celery, chopped

half bulb of garlic, crushed

1 sprig rosemary

1 sprig thyme

150ml (¼ pint) red wine

900ml (2 pints) beef stock

mashed potato, to serve
  (optional)

Pre-heat the oven to 150C/300F/Gas 2.

Heat a large frying pan and, when hot, add the dripping or oil. Seal the beef on all sides, seasoning as you do so, then transfer the beef to a large, deep saucepan.

Using the same frying pan, colour the vegetables, garlic and herbs, then add them to the meat. Pour in the red wine and enough stock to cover the meat. Cover the pan with a tight-fitting lid or foil and cook in the pre-heated oven for about 4 hours. Remove from the oven and leave in a cool place overnight.

Next morning, remove any fat from the surface and gently re-heat on top of the stove. Remove the meat and vegetables and set aside on a baking tray. Strain the liquid into another large pan, then simmer until it has reduced by at least half and the flavour has intensified.

To serve, cover the meat and vegetables with foil and re-heat in the oven at 180C/350F/Gas 4 for about 20 minutes. Serve it whole or sliced, with some of the vegetables and plenty of sauce. Mashed potato is my favourite accompaniment.

Pork Fillet with Marsala Prunes and Sweet Mustard Sauce

Here in East Anglia we have some excellent pig farmers, so it's a shame people don't eat pork more often; nowadays the meat is much leaner than it used to be. This recipe proves that you don't have to use a large joint that takes hours to cook – these fillets take a matter of minutes.

Serves 6

12-18 ready-to-eat Agen
  prunes

75ml (3fl oz) Marsala

2 fillets of pork, each about
  450g (1lb)

25ml (1fl oz) olive oil

25g (1oz) salted butter

Sweet Mustard Sauce (*see*
  page 67)

salt and pepper

Soak the prunes in the Marsala overnight.

Trim the pork fillets of any fat and sinews, then cut them into 2.5cm (1 inch) thick noisettes. (You will get about 10 good-sized noisettes out of each fillet.)

Pre-heat the oven to 200C/400F/Gas 6.

Heat a non-stick frying pan until hot, then add the oil followed by the butter. Once the butter is foaming, add the noisettes in batches, being careful not to overcrowd the pan. As each batch is sealed and coloured lightly on both sides, transfer them to a trivet placed in a roasting tin and season. Roast in the pre-heated oven for about 8 minutes.

Meanwhile, heat the sweet mustard sauce in a saucepan, add the soaked prunes and check the seasoning.

To serve, divide the noisettes among the serving plates. Spoon a little sweet mustard sauce over each plate, making sure that each person gets their share of the prunes. Serve any remaining sauce separately

Properly Garnished Roast Hen Pheasant

I've become keen on shooting in the past two years and find that people in this neck of the woods have very strong views as to how long pheasants should be hung. I prefer not to hang mine for so long that they walk themselves to the table and reckon that a week is the optimum time. Traditionally roasted pheasant with game chips, bread sauce, fried breadcrumbs and streaky bacon is still my favourite way of serving this bird. To make game chips, simply slice a large potato wafer-thin with a mandolin, then deep-fry it in about 2.5cm (1 inch) hot oil till golden brown. Drain on kitchen paper to serve. I have specified hen birds because they are usually more tender, but you can, of course, use cock pheasants instead.

Serves 4

2 hen pheasants, plucked
  and dressed (retain the
  giblets for the gravy)
1 carrot, peeled and chopped
1 small onion, peeled and
  chopped
1 stick of celery, chopped
2 cloves of garlic, peeled and
  chopped
1 bouquet garni
1 glass of red wine, plus a
  splash for deglazing the
  roasting tin
50g (2oz) softened butter
2 shallots, peeled
2 sprigs of thyme
8 thin slices of smoked fatty
  streaky bacon
beef dripping (optional)
8 chipolatas
4 slices of stale bread,
  crusts removed
1 tbsp redcurrant jelly
  (optional)
salt and pepper
bread sauce and game
  chips, to serve

Begin by making the stock for the gravy. Place the giblets in a saucepan along with the carrot, onion, celery, garlic, bouquet garni and the red wine. Add water to cover, bring to the boil and simmer very gently for 4 hours. Strain and set aside to cool, then skim off any fat.

Pre-heat the oven to 180C/350F/Gas 4.

Place the pheasants on a trivet in a roasting tin. Place half the butter, shallot and some thyme in the cavity of each pheasant. Cover the breasts with the bacon and smear with some beef dripping, if using.

Season well with salt and pepper and place in the oven. Roast for about 30 minutes, then remove the bacon and set it aside. Add the chipolatas and continue to cook the pheasants for a further 30 minutes, then insert a skewer or sharp knife into the thigh to see if the juices run clear. If they do, remove the pheasants from the oven and keep them in a warm place.

While the pheasants are roasting, make the fried breadcrumbs. Blitz the bread in a food processor until fine. Heat a little fat from the pheasant roasting tin in a heavy-based frying pan, then add the breadcrumbs and fry over a medium heat, stirring frequently, until golden.

Make the gravy. Pour off any remaining fat from the roasting tin. Add a splash of red wine to the roasting tin and bring to the boil on the top of the stove, giving the bottom and sides of the roasting tin a good scraping with a wooden spoon as you do so. Boil until reduced by about two-thirds, then pour in the giblet stock. Continue to boil and reduce until the flavour has intensified. Season, adding the redcurrant jelly, if liked.

To serve, slice the pheasant breast on to a plate with some thigh meat, bacon, chipolatas and bread sauce. Sprinkle over the breadcrumbs and, finally, pour over some gravy. Serve with game chips (or potato crisps).

Roast Breast of Guinea Fowl with Field Mushroom Stuffing

I usually steer clear of 'cheffy' recipes at home, but the succulent texture and flavour of the guinea fowl makes this one well worth making for a special occasion. You can also prepare the breasts in advance, giving yourself less work to do on the day. Spring cabbage, leeks and new potatoes go really well with this dish, as do a few lightly dressed salad leaves.

Serves 6

2 tbsp olive oil, plus extra for the guinea fowl

4 flat field mushrooms, finely chopped

1 corn-fed chicken breast, skin removed and roughly chopped

1 egg white

150ml (¼ pint) double cream

6 guinea fowl breasts, with the skin on

a knob of salted butter

salt and pepper

Heat a frying pan, add the olive oil and quickly sauté the mushrooms. Transfer to a plate and allow to cool completely. Place the chicken breast in the bowl of a food processor and, while processing, add the egg white. Continue to process until smooth. Scrape the mixture into a bowl and season with salt and pepper.

Using a spatula, slowly add enough double cream to achieve a dropping consistency, beating well between each addition. Fold the cooled mushrooms into the chicken and cream mixture to make the stuffing and then place in the fridge until required.

Make an incision with the point of a sharp knife through the thickest part of each guinea fowl breast along its length. Twist the knife to create a cavity inside each breast. Spoon the stuffing into a piping bag, then pipe as much as possible through each incision.

Pre-heat the oven to 200C/400F/Gas 6.

Heat a frying pan until hot; then add a splash of olive oil followed by a knob of salted butter. Once the butter is foaming, add the guinea fowl breasts to the pan, skin side down, turning them until sealed and coloured on both sides. Leave to cool for 15 minutes.

Place the guinea fowl breasts on a trivet, season and roast in the oven for 20-25 minutes, depending on the size of the breasts, until firm to the touch. Leave them to rest for a few minutes in a warm place, then cut into slices to serve.

Roast Goose

Goose is my favourite of the poultry family. At home we are really spoilt for choice, with a Norfolk Black turkey on Christmas Day then roast goose on Boxing Day. You need to cook the goose for long enough to achieve very flavoursome meat with a wonderful crisp skin. Remember that goose is extremely rich, so you only need to serve small portions – just as well, as a large bird serves relatively few people. Ideally the stock for the gravy should be made a day in advance and allowed to cool, making it much easier to skim off any fat.

Serves 6 generously

1 goose, weighing about 5kg
  (11lb) dressed weight
1 onion, 1 carrot and a few
  fresh sage leaves (optional)
salt and pepper

For the gravy

25g (1oz) goose fat
1 medium onion, peeled and
  chopped
2 carrots, peeled and
  chopped
1 large stick of celery,
  chopped
2 cloves of garlic, peeled and
  chopped
1 sprig of rosemary
1 sprig of thyme
the giblets from the goose
  (gizzard, neck bone,
  chopped, heart and liver)
2 tbsp red wine vinegar
1 tbsp soft brown sugar
150ml (¼ pint) red wine
900ml (2 pints) chicken
  stock
1 tbsp redcurrant jelly
salt and pepper

The day before, make the stock. In a frying pan, melt the goose fat, then colour the vegetables, garlic and herbs.

Using a slotted spoon, transfer them to a large, deep saucepan, then fry the rinsed gizzard, neck bone and heart in the remaining goose fat residue until coloured. Add them to the pan with the vegetables.

Pour the red wine vinegar into the frying pan, sprinkle over the sugar and scrape the pan; add the red wine to deglaze. Bring to the boil and simmer until reduced by half. Add this to the vegetables and giblets.

Pour in the chicken stock, bring to the boil and simmer very gently for at least I hour. Cool overnight. Next day skim any fat from the surface, return to a large saucepan and bring to a rapid boil. Reduce by at least half to intensify the flavour. Set aside.

Pre-heat the oven to 220C/425F/Gas 7.

Remove all the fat from the cavity of the goose and keep it for rendering down and freezing (it's perfect for roasting potatoes). Wash the goose thoroughly inside and out and dry completely.

Rub plenty of salt and pepper on to the breast and place the goose on a trivet in a roasting tin so that the fat will run into the pan during cooking. Place the onion, carrot and sage inside the cavity, if liked.

Place the goose in the pre-heated oven. Roast for 20 minutes, then turn the temperature down to 180C/350F/Gas 4 and continue to roast for a further 2 hrs and 20 minutes, pouring off any fat from the roasting tin from time to time. (If the goose starts to brown too early, cover it very loosely with foil, removing this for the last 20 minutes so the skin browns well.)

Leave the goose to rest for 15-20 minutes before carving.

Just before serving, chop the liver and quickly fry in a pan with a little goose fat. Reheat the gravy and add the redcurrant jelly and liver to serve.

Roast Sirloin of Beef on the Bone

The trend these days is to buy and cook beef off the bone, but to my mind you get much more flavour from a joint cooked on the bone. It does take a little longer to cook, but you have the advantage of being able to use the bone to make stock. Some people prefer to have the fillet left intact. If you do so, remove the fillet from the sirloin after 40 minutes' cooking to give you rare fillet of beef. What to serve with the best sirloin of beef? Chips, of course!

Serves 8 generously

1 piece of sirloin left on the
  bone, about 4.5-5.4kg
  (10-12lb) and 30cm
  (12 inches) long

2 medium onions

2 carrots

1 leek

1 stick celery

½ bulb garlic, skin left on
  and roughly chopped

1 sprig rosemary

2 tbsp mild curry powder

salt and pepper

Pre-heat the oven to 230C/450F/Gas 8.

Trim some of the fat from the sirloin. Roughly chop all the vegetables, leaving the skin on, and place, with the garlic and rosemary, in a large roasting tin, sitting the sirloin on top. Season well with salt and pepper and liberally sprinkle over the curry powder (this acts as a wonderful seasoning but doesn't give you curried beef!).

Place on the middle shelf of the oven and roast for 30 minutes, then turn the oven temperature down to 180C/350F/Gas 4. Cook for a further 1 hour for rare beef or 1 hour 15 minutes for medium beef.

When the beef is cooked, remove from the oven and allow to stand for 15 minutes before carving.

Roast Tournedos of Venison with Gravy

Our butcher in Wells, Arthur Howell, gets wonderful venison from the nearby Holkham Estate from roe or fallow deer. Try to find this venison, rather than meat from red deer, as the tournedos are smaller, more tender and not quite as 'gamey tasting'. I reckon venison needs to be served at least medium-rare, erring on the side of rare, but that's up to you. The gravy can be made in advance and re-heated when needed.

Serves 6

700g (1½lb) boned loin of venison, all sinew and fat removed (keep the bones)

3 tbsp olive oil, plus extra for the venison

2 onions, chopped

1 carrot, chopped

1 stick of celery, chopped

½ bulb garlic, sliced

6 juniper berries

2 sprigs of thyme

2 tbsp red wine vinegar

1 glass red wine

1.2 litres (2 pints) chicken stock

1 tbsp redcurrant jelly

a knob of butter

salt and pepper

Pre-heat the oven 200C/400F/Gas 6.

Begin by making the gravy. Place the venison bones and any trimmings into a roasting tin and roast in the oven for about 30 minutes (do not allow the bones to brown too much).

While the bones are roasting, heat a large frying pan over a medium heat. Add the olive oil, then lightly fry the vegetables, garlic, juniper berries and thyme. Transfer them to a large saucepan. When the venison bones are roasted, add them to the saucepan with the vegetables.

Pour the vinegar and wine into the roasting tin, give it a good scrape round and then, over a high heat, bring to the boil and reduce to about 4 tablespoonfuls of liquid. Add this to the pan with the vegetables and bones. Pour in the chicken stock then bring to boil and reduce by half.

Strain the reduced liquid into another saucepan, stir in the redcurrant jelly then boil again to reduce, until the flavour has intensified. Remove from the heat and set aside.

Pre-heat the oven to 200C/400F/Gas 6.

Cut the venison loin into 8 tournedos, each about 3cm (1½ inches) thick.

Heat a frying pan until hot. Add a splash of olive oil and a knob of butter, then seal the tournedos on both sides, seasoning with salt and pepper as you do so. Transfer them to a trivet placed in a roasting tin, then roast in the oven for 10-15 minutes.

Remove the venison from the oven, allow to rest for a few minutes. Serve with the re-heated gravy, Parmentier Potatoes and Celeriac and Slowly Braised Red Cabbage, (see pages 164 and 184).

Roasted Corn-fed Chicken with Lemon and Parma Ham

Making the sauce in the roasting tin in which you have cooked the chicken maximises its lemony flavour. Serve this with young vegetables or lightly dressed salad leaves.

25ml (1fl oz) olive oil

knob of butter

4 corn-fed chicken breasts
  with the skin on

1 lemon, quartered

1 onion, peeled and chopped

1 stick of celery, chopped

4 sprigs of tarragon

275ml (½ pint) chicken stock

55ml (2fl oz) whipping cream

a little sugar (optional)

4 slices Parma ham

rocket leaves (optional)

salt and pepper

Pre-heat the oven to 190C/375F/Gas 5.

Heat a frying pan till hot, then add the olive oil followed by the butter. Place the chicken breasts, skin side down, in the foaming butter, pressing them down firmly until sealed and just coloured. Turn the chicken over and lightly colour the other side, then remove from the pan and set aside.

Quickly fry the lemon quarters, together with the vegetables and tarragon, in the same pan until coloured and caramelised. Place them in a roasting tin, with the chicken breasts on top, skin side uppermost.

Roast the chicken for about 25 minutes, depending on the thickness of the chicken breasts, until the juices run clear.

Remove the chicken breasts from the tin and set aside in a warm place to rest. Pour the chicken stock into the roasting tin with the lemon quarters and vegetables, giving the pan a good scrape to loosen any bits of chicken and lemon from the base.

Bring to the boil on the hob and simmer for 10 minutes. Add the cream, then bring back to the boil. Check the seasoning, adding a little sugar if the sauce is too sharp. Pass the sauce through a sieve into another pan and heat to just below boiling point.

To serve, place one chicken breast, sliced on the bias, in the centre of each plate. Spoon over some sauce, then add a slice of Parma ham and some lightly dressed rocket leaves, if liked.

Salad of Lamb with Artichokes and Hazelnut Dressing

Lamb and hazelnuts complement each other perfectly; here, I particularly like the combination of hot lamb and artichokes with cold salad leaves and dressing. This dish makes an unusual main course for 4, but it could also be served as a starter for 6 people. Sautéed Jerusalem artichokes work wonderfully well here, but if you can't find them, use new potatoes instead.

Serves 4-6

40g (1½oz) whole, skinned
  hazelnuts

1 tbsp Dijon mustard, plus
  1 tsp for the dressing

1 tsp red wine vinegar

½ tsp runny honey

120ml (4fl oz) olive oil

juice of ½ lime

275g (10oz) Jerusalem
  artichokes, peeled and kept
  in water with a little lemon
  juice added

olive oil and butter for frying
  the artichokes and lamb

2 racks of lamb, taken off
  the bone and all fat
  removed

a selection of young salad
  leaves, such as rocket, ruby
  chard, frisée, lollo rosso
  and chervil

salt and pepper

Pre-heat the oven to 180C/350F/Gas 4.

Place the hazelnuts on a baking tray and roast in the oven for about 15 minutes until golden-brown. Remove from the oven and when cool, blitz in a food processor.

Make the dressing. In a bowl, mix together 1 tsp mustard, vinegar and honey, then slowly whisk in the olive oil and lime juice. Taste and season. Add 1 tbsp of the ground hazelnuts.

Transfer the artichokes to a pan of salted water, then bring to the boil and simmer till they are just cooked. Remove from the heat and refresh the artichokes under cold water, then slice them.

Heat some oil in a frying pan, then add some butter. When the butter is foaming, sauté the artichokes on a high heat, turning them from time to time, until lightly coloured. Using a slotted spoon, remove from the frying pan, place on a baking tray, season and set aside.

Wipe out the pan and, still on a high heat, add a little more oil and butter. Seal the racks of lamb until well coloured. Remove from the frying pan and sit them on a trivet in a roasting tin. Paint each rack with mustard. Put the remaining ground hazelnuts on a plate and press the mustard-coated racks into them. (You can prepare the recipe ahead to this stage.)

When you are ready to cook the lamb, pre-heat the oven to 200C/400F/Gas 6.

Roast the lamb for 20 minutes, reheating the artichokes at the same time on a lower shelf. Allow the lamb to rest for a few minutes before cutting into slices.

To serve, arrange a pile of sautéed artichokes in the centre of each plate and top each one with some slices of lamb. Place some salad leaves on top and spoon the dressing over.

Steak and Kidney Pudding

Traditional and hearty, there is something comforting and satisfying about eating really good steak and kidney pudding – one where the very rich gravy oozes out as soon as you put the knife in – on a winter's day. Don't prepare the suet crust in advance: simply make the pastry, fill the pudding and cook it or the crust will be soggy. Mashed potatoes and Savoy cabbage make superb accompaniments.

Serves 6

For the suet crust pastry

350g (12oz) self-raising flour

175g (6oz) shredded
  beef suet

a generous pinch of salt

butter, for greasing the
  pudding basin and
  greaseproof paper

For the filling

500g (1lb 2oz) chuck steak,
  trimmed and diced into
  2.5cm (1 inch) pieces

225g (8oz) best beef
  kidneys, diced

50g (2oz) seasoned flour

25g (1oz) lard or dripping

175g (6oz) field mushrooms,
  cut into chunks

1 large shallot, finely sliced

1 tbsp chopped parsley

50ml (2fl oz) red wine

225ml (8fl oz) beef stock

salt and pepper

1.75 litre (3 pint) pudding
basin, lightly buttered

Make the pastry. In a large bowl, mix together the flour, suet and salt. Add about 225ml (8fl oz) water, or enough to form a soft dough that doesn't stick to your fingers. Turn the dough on to a lightly floured surface and knead briefly until smooth.

Roll the dough out into a large circle about 37.5cm (15 inches) in diameter. Cut out a quarter of the circle and set this piece aside to use later for the top of the pudding. Line the buttered pudding basin with the remaining pastry, overlapping the cut edges and sealing them with a little water so that they stick together.

Make the filling. Toss the steak and kidney in the seasoned flour. Heat a frying pan until hot, then add the lard or dripping. Seal the steak and kidney, turning to colour well. (You may need to do this in several batches to avoid overcrowding the pan.) Transfer the meat to a large bowl. Add the mushrooms and shallot to the same pan and sauté quickly until soft.

Add the mushrooms and shallot to the bowl and season well. Add the chopped parsley and mix well, then place it all in the pastry-lined pudding basin. Mix the red wine and stock together, and pour in enough to just cover the meat.

Roll out the reserved piece of pastry so that it will generously cover the top of the basin. Brush the edge with water, press it firmly over the top of the pudding, then crimp the edges together well to seal the pudding. Place a piece of buttered paper on top of the suet crust, then cover the top of the bowl with muslin and tie securely.

Steam the pudding in a large double boiler with a tight-fitting lid for about 4 hours, not forgetting to keep the water topped up. Allow the pudding to stand for a few minutes, then carefully remove the muslin and paper. Run a knife round the edge of the pudding, then turn it out on to a large plate and serve immediately.

Vegetables

Locally sourced, seasonal produce, as fresh as you can get, cooked as quickly as possible until just tender is my 'mantra' when it comes to serving vegetables. The four or five types of vegetable on offer with dinner at Morston are always carefully chosen to complement the meat or fish they're served with.

For freshness and real flavour, local sourcing is crucial. One of our suppliers, from nearby Holt, grows the most wonderful young salad leaves, wild garlic and courgette flowers for us (the latter deep fry brilliantly in tempura batter with a little Parmesan grated over them). Another small farmer grows finger-length carrots, young leeks, beetroots and wonderful large Norfolk Pink Potatoes which are great for roasting (though not so good for mashing).

A chapter on vegetables and Norfolk would be incomplete without reference to our sublime local asparagus and samphire. It's sad that these wonderful ingredients have such a short season – the samphire starts as the asparagus season draws to a close – so we serve them daily when we can.

On the other hand, the season for some vegetables is now much longer than it used to be. We can get new potatoes and broad beans in May; fresh peas are also available much earlier than they used to be and purple sprouting broccoli is still around in August.

But why is seasonality so important? First, a lot of imported, 'out of English season' vegetables have little flavour and are no longer really fresh by the time they reach the supermarket shelves. Secondly, eating produce in season still retains a huge amount of thrill and anticipation for me.

I love autumn and winter vegetables too, when the more robust red cabbage, parsnips and swede come into their own – especially once they've had a frost on them. Yet I have to admit that, usually by February, I start to look forward to all the spring vegetables that will soon be in season again.

The preparation and cooking of vegetables in this country has improved so dramatically that it's now possible to wow even the most committed carnivore with imaginative, appetising and colourful vegetarian food, and in this I believe Britain is ahead of our European counterparts; it always disappoints me how few vegetables are served at good restaurants in France.

When boiling vegetables, I follow a rule of thumb that was often quoted in my mother's day and has been repeated by guests at my cookery demonstrations: vegetables grown above ground should be dropped into boiling, salted water; vegetables grown in the ground should be placed into cold, salted water and brought up to the boil.

It's time we all made more the wonderful native produce available to us, maximising its flavour, nutritional value and colour in our cooking. That's what I aim to do in this chapter.

Bashed New Potatoes

This recipe (*see* right) gives another dimension to new potatoes. It is a good way to cook them when they are past that initial flush of 'newness' and are too big to serve whole. There is a lot of butter here, so offer small portions – but, then again, anything to do with new potatoes needs plenty of butter!

Serves 8

900g (2lb) English new
 potatoes, scraped and cut
 into chunks

3 tbsp mint, stalks and
 leaves separated

225g (8oz) salted butter

4 tbsp single cream

salt and pepper

Place the potatoes in a saucepan with enough water to cover them completely. Add the stalks from the mint and a good pinch of salt.

Bring the potatoes to the boil and cook until very soft. Drain well, then return them to the pan. Off the heat, add the butter and, using a wooden spoon, bash the potatoes well to break them up. Season with salt and pepper, add the cream and mix well. Finally, stir in the finely chopped mint leaves to serve.

Parmentier Potatoes and Celeriac

Potatoes and celeriac make a wonderful combination and in this recipe they are fried. Cooking them this way is lethal, though – once I find myself picking at them in the pan I can never stop as they are so delicious.

Serves 6

275g (10oz) potatoes, peeled
 and cut into small, even-
 sized dice

275g (10oz) celeriac, peeled
 and cut into small, even-
 sized dice

3 tbsp olive oil

40g (1½oz) butter

½ bulb of garlic, the cloves
 peeled and roughly
 chopped

a sprig of rosemary

salt and pepper

Mix the potatoes and celeriac together.

Heat the oil and butter in a frying pan over a medium heat. Add the potatoes, celeriac, garlic and rosemary. Season with salt and pepper.

Fry the potatoes and celeriac, keeping them moving as they start to colour. When they are cooked, drain in a sieve or on kitchen paper and serve immediately.

Braised Leeks with Gruyère

Young leeks are a more stylish choice for presentation, but this recipe works just as well with full-sized ones. You can prepare the leeks in advance, re-heating them to serve; if you do this, refresh them under cold, running water as soon as they are cooked, then drain thoroughly. Oven-roasted Tomato Fondue with Garlic and Thyme (*see* page 174) goes really well with this dish: together they would make a wonderful vegetarian supper.

Serves 6

24 young leeks, trimmed to
  equal lengths

75g (3oz) Gruyère cheese,
  finely grated

salt and pepper

a well-buttered gratin dish

Bring a large pan of salted water to the boil. Drop in the young leeks and boil till just tender, literally a few minutes (I often cook an extra one to test while they are cooking). Drain thoroughly and lay them in a single layer in a buttered gratin dish.

Sprinkle over the grated Gruyère, season and either allow the heat from the leeks to melt the cheese or place the dish under a pre-heated grill for a few seconds until bubbling and golden in colour.

Gratin of White Turnips

Turnips tend not to feature too often in many people's repertoires, yet this is a great way to prepare them (*see* right). What's more, they can be prepared well ahead then re-heated. Make sure you buy firm-fleshed turnips.

Serves 6-8

900g (2lb) firm white turnips

425ml (¾ pint) whipping
  cream

3 cloves of garlic, grated

freshly grated nutmeg

25g (1oz) freshly grated
  Parmesan

salt and pepper

a well-buttered gratin dish
and some greaseproof paper

Pre-heat the oven to 170C/325F/Gas 3.

Peel the turnips, then slice them as thinly as possible (this is best done with a mandolin) and place in a large bowl. Pour in the cream and garlic. Add some gratings of nutmeg, season with pepper and a little salt, then mix thoroughly.

Layer the turnip slices in the buttered gratin dish and carefully pour in any remaining cream mixture. Cover with greaseproof paper and cook for 1 hour. Remove the greaseproof paper and scatter the Parmesan over. Return to the oven for a further 30 minutes, or until the turnips are very soft, the cream has thickened and the gratin has browned.

Braised Puy Lentils with Parsley

The lentils in this dish retain some 'bite', making them the perfect complement to fish such as haddock or cod. If serving them with fish, I would use fish stock instead of chicken. Vegetarians could use water or, better still, vegetable stock (nage).

Serves 6

225g (8oz) Puy lentils

75g (3oz) butter

25g (1oz) carrot, peeled and
   finely diced

25g (1oz) celery, finely diced

25g (1oz) onion, peeled and
   finely chopped

1 clove of garlic, peeled and
   grated

425ml (¾ pint) chicken stock

3 tbsp finely chopped fresh
   parsley

2 tbsp snipped chives

salt and pepper

Wash the lentils thoroughly and leave to drain in a sieve.

Melt the butter in a saucepan, then add all the vegetables and garlic. Cook over a medium heat, stirring occasionally, until the vegetables are just starting to soften. Add the lentils and cook for a further 2-3 minutes.

Pour in the chicken stock, cover and continue to cook on a very low simmer until the lentils are soft but not mushy and the stock has been absorbed. Just before serving, stir in the herbs and season to taste.

Buttered Samphire

It always amazes me how much London shops charge for samphire. It is cooked like asparagus and, similarly, has a short season – from the end of June through to August.

Serves 6

450g (1lb) fresh samphire,
  thoroughly rinsed

1 tbsp sugar

50g (2oz) unsalted butter

good-quality aged balsamic
  vinegar

freshly ground black pepper

Bring a large saucepan of water to the boil. Drop in the samphire and add the sugar. Boil for 2 minutes, then taste a sprig to see if it is cooked (the fleshy end should slip off the stem easily).

Drain the samphire thoroughly, smear with the butter and transfer to a warmed dish. Drizzle over a little balsamic vinegar and season with pepper. Serve immediately.

Cauliflower Purée with White Truffle Oil

This is the lightest of purées (*see* right), which I often serve warm as an accompaniment to meat and fish dishes, or cold in a canapé tartlet with tiny sautéed girolles mushrooms. To make it seriously luxurious and indulgent, add a splash of white truffle oil.

Serves 6

1 medium cauliflower

570ml (1 pint) full-fat milk

freshly grated nutmeg

10g (½oz) salted butter

2 tsp white truffle oil
  (optional)

salt and pepper

Remove the outer green leaves from the cauliflower, then break the white florets into pieces. Place these in a saucepan, add the milk and, over a moderate heat, bring to the boil. Cover and cook until the cauliflower is very tender.

Carefully pour the cauliflower and milk into a blender and process until you get a really light, smooth purée. Season with freshly grated nutmeg, salt and pepper, then add butter and truffle oil, if using.

Purple Sprouting Broccoli with Hollandaise Sauce and Crispy Bacon

In my kitchen, purple sprouting broccoli – which heralds the longer, warmer days of spring – is treated with nearly as much reverence as asparagus. Simplicity is the key: all it really needs is melted butter, salt and freshly ground black pepper. For a special occasion, however, I like to add crispy bacon and spoon over some hollandaise sauce.

Serves 4

450g (1lb) fresh purple
  sprouting broccoli,
  preferably Norfolk-grown

8 rashers smoked streaky
  bacon, fried to a crisp

1 quantity Hollandaise Sauce
  (*see* page 64)

salt and freshly ground
  black pepper

Trim any tough stalks from the purple sprouting broccoli, much as if you were preparing asparagus.

Bring a large saucepan of salted water to the boil and drop in the broccoli. Cook for a few minutes only until the stalks are just tender (test with the point of a knife as if you were testing a new potato).

Drain the broccoli immediately, giving it a good grinding of salt and pepper. Serve with the crispy bacon and some hollandaise sauce.

Fiery Red Onions

This is good served cold with barbecued meat dishes. If you prefer less heat, use the larger, milder chillies, adding them gradually and tasting as you go. When slicing the onions, try to keep the slices intact for a better colour. Cooking the onions on a ridged frying pan (*see* right) gives a very appetising appearance but if you don't have one, use a normal frying pan, making sure they are well coloured on both sides.

Serves 6

6 medium red onions, peeled
  and cut into slices about
  5mm (¼ inch) thick
4 tbsp olive oil
1 eating apple, peeled, cored
  and diced
2 tbsp peeled, chopped
  cucumber
2 chillies, deseeded and
  finely chopped
4 tbsp freshly chopped
  coriander
juice of 2 limes
1 heaped tsp soft brown
  sugar
1 tbsp soy sauce
1 tsp Thai fish sauce
  (optional)
salt and pepper

Place the onion slices in a bowl and pour over the olive oil. Heat a ridged frying pan until hot, add the onion slices and griddle for about 4 minutes on each side until well coloured.

Transfer the onions to another bowl, carefully mixing in the remaining ingredients (don't worry if the onions break up at this stage). Taste and season before serving.

Oven-roasted Tomato Fondue with Garlic and Thyme

One of our favourite recipes at Morston, this thick, chunky sauce is fantastic with meat and fish dishes. Slow oven cooking really intensifies the flavour of the tomatoes. Ring the changes by adding freshly torn basil and melting cheese on top just before serving.

Serves 6

700g (1½lb) vine tomatoes,
  skinned, deseeded and
  diced
55ml (2fl oz) olive oil
2 shallots, finely chopped
4 whole cloves of garlic
sprig of fresh thyme
salt and pepper

Pre-heat the oven to 150C/300F/Gas 2.

Mix all the ingredients together, then spread them evenly over a large baking tray. Put it in the oven and leave to cook for about 1 hour, by which time the moisture will have evaporated and the tomatoes will have started to dry out a little.

Serve warm or cold with fish or barbecue dishes.

Mashed Parsley Potatoes

You must try this, adapted from a recipe kindly given to me by one of our finest cookery writers, Simon Hopkinson. Whenever he stays at Morston we inevitably end up talking about food and I never cease to be impressed by his amazing knowledge. This dish can be made in advance and re-heated when needed – it has a lovely vibrant green colour and silky-smooth texture.

Serves 6-8

900g (2lb) large baking
  potatoes, scrubbed

110g (4oz) flat-leaf parsley,
  leaves stripped from the
  stalks

110g (4oz) butter

150ml (¼ pint) milk

150ml (¼ pint) whipping
  cream

1 clove of garlic, peeled and
  roughly chopped

salt and pepper

Pre-heat the oven to 200C/400F/Gas 6.

Place the potatoes in the pre-heated oven and bake until soft.

Blanch the parsley leaves by plunging them into boiling water for 1½ minutes. Refresh them immediately under cold, running water, drain well and place in a blender.

In another saucepan, heat together the butter, milk, cream and garlic. While still hot, pour this mixture into the blender with the parsley. Process for 3-4 minutes to allow the colour to develop.

Halve the potatoes, scoop out the flesh and press it through a sieve into a bowl. Add the warm parsley purée, mix thoroughly and season with salt and pepper. Keep warm until ready to serve.

Potato and Wild Mushroom Dauphinoise

This is a really good variation of the traditional potatoes Dauphinoise. The secret is to make sure you are really generous with the middle layer of mushrooms. A brilliant accompaniment for game dishes, this can be made in advance and re-heated when needed.

Serves 8

900g (2lb) old waxy
  potatoes, preferably Maris
  Piper
120ml (4fl oz) milk
425ml (¾ pint) double cream
freshly grated nutmeg
3 tbsp olive oil
6 shallots, peeled and thinly
  sliced
275g (10oz) mixed wild
  mushrooms
salt and pepper

a deep-sided roasting tin or
gratin dish and greaseproof
paper

Pre-heat the oven to 180C/350F/Gas 4.

Using a mandolin, thinly slice the potatoes into a large bowl. Pour over the milk and cream, season with salt, pepper and nutmeg, then mix well and set aside.

Heat the oil in a frying pan, then fry the shallots until soft and lightly coloured. Spread them over the base of a deep-sided roasting tin or gratin dish. Next, fry the wild mushrooms, then set aside.

Spread half the potato and cream mixture over the shallots. Cover with the mushrooms, then the remaining potatoes. Carefully pour over any milk and cream left in the bowl.

Cover the potatoes with greaseproof paper and cook in the oven for 1 hour. Remove the greaseproof paper and return to the oven for a further 30 minutes to allow them to colour. Check that the potatoes are cooked by piercing with a sharp knife, then serve or set aside to re-heat later.

How to roast peppers

Everyone has their own way of removing skins from peppers. This method ensures the skins are wrinkled enough to remove, although some people prefer to place them under a grill or even use a blow torch. Oil and garlic are optional; if I am using the skinned peppers for Peperonata or Summer Salsa (*see* pages 90 and 96 respectively), I might add some olive oil and garlic, but really it is up to you. I'm not giving quantities here – see individual recipes for details.

Pre-heat the oven to 220C/425F/Gas 7.

Lightly oil a baking tray. Halve the peppers, remove the seeds and place them cut side down on the baking tray. Drizzle with oil and grate over some garlic (optional). Season with salt and pepper.

Place the peppers in the oven on a low shelf and cook for 10 minutes. Turn the tray round and cook for a further 10 minutes. By this stage, the skins of the peppers may be sufficiently wrinkled but should not be charred or shrunken.

Remove the peppers from the oven, place them in a bowl and cover with clingfilm. After a few minutes, the steaming effect will allow you to slip the skins off easily.

Sautéed Jerusalem Artichokes with Onions and Parsley

This makes a great alternative to sautéed potatoes. The artichokes can be cooked in advance, transferred to a baking tray and then re-heated in a moderate oven (180C/350F/Gas 4) for 10-15 minutes before adding the freshly chopped parsley. If you want to peel the artichokes in advance, keep them in a bowl of water with the juice of half a lemon added to prevent discolouring.

Serves 6

450g (1lb) Jerusalem
artichokes

2 tbsp olive oil

25g (1oz) butter

I medium onion, peeled and
finely chopped

salt and pepper

4 tbsp freshly chopped
parsley, to serve

Peel the Jerusalem artichokes and place them in a pan of cold salted water. Bring to the boil and cook until just tender, then remove from the heat and refresh under cold running water. Slice the cooled artichokes and set aside.

Heat a frying pan over a medium heat. Add the olive oil followed by the butter and fry the onion until just soft. Add the artichokes, turning them as they cook, until they are golden on each side. Season with salt and pepper and add the parsley just before serving.

Slowly Braised Red Cabbage

I like braised red cabbage to be soft and pappy and for that reason it is probably better prepared a day in advance. This recipe comes from Toby, who has been at Morston for six years, working his way up to become an integral part of the team and a very talented chef. If he starts on it as soon as he gets to work in the early afternoon, we can serve it in the evening for dinner at 8pm. Red cabbage goes really well with goose and game.

Serves 8

110g (4oz) butter

1 red cabbage, centre core
   removed and thinly sliced

1 cinnamon stick

2 cloves

2 star anise

110g (4oz) dark brown sugar

juice of 1 orange, plus zest
   of ½ orange

1 x 75cl bottle red wine

salt and pepper

Pre-heat the oven to 150C/300F/Gas 2.

Melt the butter in a heavy-based saucepan and sauté the cabbage until it has softened. Remove from the heat and set aside.

Place the remaining ingredients in another saucepan, bring to the boil and simmer for 10 minutes. Pass this mixture through a sieve, adding it to the red cabbage. Cover the pan with a lid, bring to the boil, then place in the oven and braise for a minimum of 3 hours.

Transfer the saucepan to the stove top. Remove the lid and, over a medium heat, reduce the liquid, leaving just enough to coat the cabbage.

Puddings

Chocolate puddings, cheesecakes, sponge puddings, syrupy puddings, sticky meringues, ice creams, fruit puddings, tarts and pastries, pancakes and soufflés: I love them all! This chapter was the most difficult one to write – not because I couldn't decide what to include, but rather because I had to leave some of my favourite recipes out. One thing's for sure: I could write an entire book on puddings.

Since the publication of my first book, I have constantly found myself thinking 'I must put that in book two' every time we put a new dessert on the menu. I hope such offerings as my cheesecake and peach melba excite you as much as they excite me. Puddings leave your guests with a final impression of your cooking, which may be why some chefs over-egg the pudding with elaborate, caramel cages and sparklers. In the past, I have been there, done it and maybe even got the T shirt, but these days I believe it's much more impressive to serve a pudding that is spot on in its own right.

These recipes range from the wickedly decadent to the classic, with highlights including Chocolate Torte (very rich, but you only need a tiny sliver of it); Passion Fruit Tart which has an intensity of flavour that makes it well worth the effort, and Soufflé Rothschild (don't be wary of trying this one, as it's a real show stopper). These indulgent puddings make wonderful dinner party desserts, especially as many of them can be made in advance.

There are quite a few ice cream recipes and if you're new to making them yourself, then you're in for a treat. If ice creams and sorbets become a regular part of your repertoire (and we make them every day at Morston), buy a proper ice cream machine with a built-in freezing unit. Of course, you can put a custard-based ice cream or a fruit purée sorbet in a container and into the freezer, but making it in a proper ice cream machine gives an unsurpassable texture. Remember to remove ice cream from the freezer 15 minutes before serving.

Fruit is an important component of many puddings and from May to October we enjoy top-class, locally grown strawberries, raspberries and, in recent years, blueberries. Although the use of cloches and new varieties have lengthened the strawberry season, the very best strawberries are those that are just bursting with natural, sun-ripened flavour. We also use a lot of blackcurrants, redcurrants and whitecurrants, all grown just a mile down the road from our kitchen door. Blackcurrants make the most wonderful ice cream and a fabulous hot soufflé, both of which feature on the menu at Morston. Then, just as the summer fruits are on the wane, along come the stone fruit – plums, greengages and damsons – in September, and don't forget quinces if you're lucky enough to find them, as these make the most wonderful jelly or membrillo to accompany cheese.

One thing I hope you'll take from this book is the sheer delight of making – and eating – these wonderful puddings.

Baked Vanilla Cheesecake with Poached Blueberries and Crème Fraîche

This has to be one of my favourite puddings. The filling is best mixed by hand; if you use a mixer or whisk you will incorporate too much air and spoil the texture of the cheesecake. When you take it out of the oven after 1 hour, it may still look very wobbly, but trust me, it will set. If you are really worried, stick a knife into it. If the knife comes out hot, it's time to take it out of the oven.

Serves 8 generously

For the base

110g (4oz) salted butter, softened
25g (1oz) icing sugar
110g (4oz) self-raising flour, sifted

For the filling

425g (15oz) full-fat Philadelphia cream cheese
425g (15oz) crème fraîche
250g (9oz) caster sugar
40g (1½oz) plain flour, sifted
4 eggs, beaten
65ml (2½fl oz) double cream
1 tsp vanilla extract or vanilla bean paste

For the poached blueberries

225g (8oz) blueberries
50g (2oz) caster sugar
crème fraîche, to serve

23cm (9 inch) plain-edged flan ring with a loose base, greased and lined with greaseproof paper to come 2.5cm (1 inch) above the top of the flan ring; baking tray for cooking the base

Pre-heat the oven to 190C/375F/Gas 5.

Make the biscuit base. Cream the butter and sugar together in a food mixer or with a hand-held electric whisk till white and fluffy. Still whisking, add the self-raising flour.

Spread the mixture thinly on to a greaseproof paper-lined baking tray. Place in the oven and bake for 20 minutes till golden in colour. Leave to cool on a wire rack, then blitz the biscuit in a food processor. Press the crumbs evenly and firmly into the base of the lined flan ring.

Reduce the oven temperature to 150C/300F/Gas 2.

Make the filling. In a bowl, beat together the cream cheese and crème fraîche with the caster sugar. Next beat in the plain flour, followed slowly by the eggs. When these have been incorporated, beat in the cream and vanilla extract.

Pour the mixture over the biscuit base and place on a baking tray in the lower half of the oven. Bake for 1 hour, by which time the cheesecake will be barely coloured; it should be just firm on the outside but still quite wobbly in the centre. Remove from the oven and allow to cool before placing in the fridge for several hours to firm up.

Place the blueberries, sugar and 2 tablespoons water in a saucepan and heat gently over a low heat. By the time the sugar has melted the blueberries should be softened but still whole.

Serve the cheesecake cut into slices, with poached blueberries and a good dollop of crème fraîche. If you are feeling really indulgent, this would also go well with home-made blackcurrant ice cream.

Champagne Granità

175g (6oz) caster sugar

150ml (¼ pint) water

3 tbsp lime juice

75cl bottle of Champagne

Place a non-reactive metal roasting tin, 25.5 x 30cm (10 x 12 inches) and about 2.5cm (1 inch) deep, in the freezer to chill for at least 1 hour.

In a small saucepan, bring the sugar and water to the boil until the sugar has dissolved. Cool the syrup by pouring it into a medium-sized bowl sitting in a larger bowl of iced water, stirring occasionally. When cool, add the lime juice. Very slowly stir in the Champagne, retaining as many of the bubbles as possible.

Pour the mixture into the tray in the freezer and freeze for at least 2 hours, or until ice crystals start to form round the edges. Using a fork, scrape and stir the crystals into the centre of the tin to form granità. Return the tin to the freezer and repeat this process until you have a tray of crystals.

Serve the granità immediately.

Strawberry (or Raspberry) Creams

This pudding does take a long time to cook and you will begin to wonder if it will ever set. But be patient: it will eventually reach the 'just set' stage and should never be left to become solid. Serve with a bowl of strawberries or raspberries, depending on which fruit you have used for the cream.

Serves 6

175g (6oz) strawberries, hulled, or raspberries, plus extra for serving

3 tbsp caster sugar

1 tbsp fraise (strawberry) or framboise (raspberry) liqueur (optional)

4 egg yolks

225ml (8fl oz) double cream

3 tsp icing sugar

Pre-heat the oven to 150C/300F/Gas 2.

Blitz 175g (6oz) of the fruit in a liquidiser, together with the caster sugar, liqueur and egg yolks.

Pass the mixture through a fine sieve into a bowl. Stir in the cream, then pour the mixture into individual ramekins.

Place the ramekins in a bain marie and cook in the pre-heated oven for about 1 hour. When the creams are just wobbly in the centre but on the verge of setting, remove from the oven. Leave to cool completely, then place in the fridge until needed.

About 30 minutes before serving, sprinkle the top of each cream with ½ teaspoon icing sugar then caramelise using a chef's blow torch. Serve with a separate pot of strawberries or raspberries and some Champagne Granità.

Chocolate Truffle Torte

This can be served as a frozen torte or straight from the fridge, but either way you can make it well in advance. It is very rich so serve in small quantities, maybe with some real custard (crème Anglaise, *see* page 214), and raspberries.

Serves 10

For the chocolate truffle filling

250g (9oz) good-quality
  dark chocolate

75g (3oz) caster sugar

5 egg yolks

425ml (¾ pint) double cream

For the sponges

melted butter, for greasing

6 eggs, separated

110g (4oz) caster sugar

50g (2oz) cocoa powder,
  sifted, plus extra for
  dusting

4 tbsp Tia Maria liqueur

2 x 20cm (8 inch) loose-
based sandwich tins and a
20cm (8 inch) springform
cake tin to assemble the
torte, plus greaseproof paper
for lining.

Lightly brush the base and sides of the sandwich tins with melted butter and line the base with good-quality greaseproof paper.

Make the chocolate truffle filling. Break the chocolate into small pieces and place in a food processor. Put the sugar in a pan with 7 tbsp cold water and heat gently until dissolved. Bring to the boil, being careful not to allow the liquid to colour.

Give the chocolate a quick blitz in the food processor. Then, with the motor running, pour in the hot syrup followed by the egg yolks. Process until you have a really smooth mixture, then scrape it into a large bowl.

In another bowl, whip the cream to form a soft trail. Quickly fold this into the chocolate mixture until thoroughly amalgamated and really smooth, then place the truffle filling in the fridge to firm up a little.

Pre-heat the oven to 180C/350F/Gas 4.

Make the sponges. Place the egg yolks and sugar in a food mixer and whisk on high speed for about 5 minutes until pale and doubled in volume. Next carefully whisk in the cocoa powder.

In a spotlessly clean bowl, whisk the egg whites until stiff. Using a large metal spoon, gently fold them into the egg and cocoa mixture. Divide the mixture between the sandwich tins and bake in the centre of the oven for 20 minutes (by which time the sponges should be just coming away from the sides of the tins and be springy to the touch).

Remove the sponges from the oven and turn out on to a wire rack. Trim the edges and place 1 sponge layer in the bottom of a deep-sided springform cake tin. Drizzle over 2 tbsp Tia Maria.

Remove the truffle filling from the fridge and spread it on to the sponge in the cake tin. Add the second sponge layer and drizzle the remaining Tia Maria over the top. Place the torte in the fridge, or freezer, for at least 4 hours to firm up.

Remove the torte from the fridge or freezer and take it out of the tin 15-20 minutes before serving. Dust with cocoa powder and serve with a little home-made custard and raspberries.

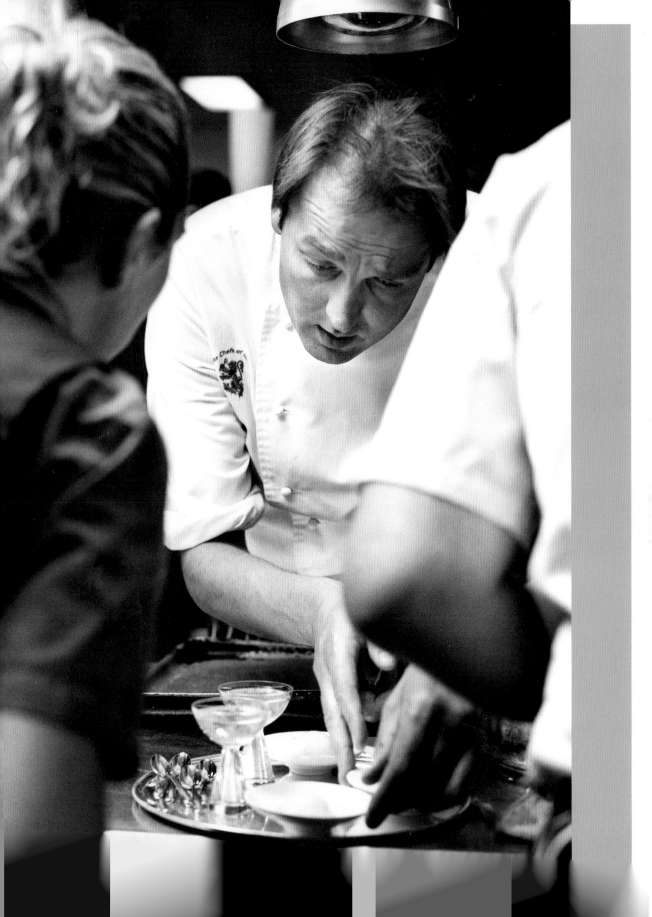

Coffee Meringue with Cream and Summer Fruits

We once served this for Delia's birthday dinner and she came back for a third helping – say no more! Everyone loves meringue and this recipe is particularly good: soft-centred, almost like a pavlova, with a crisp top. It will keep, but is best eaten on the day it is made. Surprisingly, you will obtain the most subtle flavour by using instant coffee powder (not granules).

Serves 8

75g (3oz) icing sugar

2 heaped tsp instant coffee
 powder

4 egg whites

110g (4oz) caster sugar

425ml (¾ pint) double cream

450g (1lb) summer fruits,
 such as strawberries,
 raspberries, blueberries
 and redcurrants

a large baking tray lined with
good-quality greaseproof
paper.

Pre-heat the oven to 140C/275F/Gas 1.

Sift the icing sugar and coffee powder into a bowl. Then, in another, spotlessly clean bowl, whisk the egg whites on high speed until they have increased in volume and started to stiffen. Still whisking, slowly add the caster sugar and continue to whisk until you reach the stiff-peak stage. Turn off the machine and, using a slotted metal spoon, vigorously beat in the sifted icing sugar and coffee powder until the mixture is glossy.

Spoon the meringue on to the centre of the lined baking tray and, using a palette knife, spread it into a circle about 28cm (11 inches) in diameter and 2cm (¾ inch) thick.

Place the meringue in the centre of the oven and bake for about 1½ hours, by which time it should look cracked on top but still be slightly soft in the centre. Remove from the oven, allow to cool and then carefully lift the meringue off the greaseproof paper and place on a large serving plate.

Whip the cream until it just holds, then spread it loosely over the meringue. Scatter the summer fruits liberally on top and serve.

Financiers with Chocolate Orange Centres

I've not come across any better petits fours than these dainty little French-style fairy cakes. We've always made financiers and, along the way, have fine-tuned the recipe. They really melt in the mouth, especially when served warm. The chocolate orange cream filling can be made in advance and will keep for up to a week in the fridge.

Makes 24 small financiers

For the chocolate orange filling

40g (1½oz) milk chocolate

25g (1oz) dark chocolate

65ml (2½fl oz) double cream

25ml (1fl oz) golden syrup

1 tbsp Cointreau or orange-
  flavoured liqueur

10g (½oz) unsalted butter,
  plus extra for greasing the
  muffin trays

For the financiers

110g (4oz) ground almonds

60g (2½oz) caster sugar

25g (1oz) soft plain flour,
  plus extra for dusting the
  muffin trays

3 egg whites

25ml (1fl oz) golden syrup

150g (5oz) unsalted butter

2 mini muffin trays, each
with 12 holes, lightly
buttered and floured

Make the filling. Break all the chocolate into small pieces and place in a bowl. In a saucepan, bring the cream and syrup to the boil. Pour this on to the chocolate, stirring well until it has melted.

Add the liqueur and butter, then stir vigorously until really smooth. Set aside to cool then keep in the fridge until needed.

Make the financiers. In a bowl, combine the ground almonds, sugar and flour. Add the egg whites and golden syrup, then mix thoroughly. Leave to stand for a few minutes at room temperature so that the ground almonds can absorb the moisture from the egg whites.

Pre-heat the oven to 190C/375F/Gas 5.

Place the butter in a saucepan and, over a moderate heat, bring to the boil. Cook until it is a light nut-brown colour, then set aside to cool. When it is completely cold, stir it into the rested cake mixture.

Spoon the mixture into the buttered and floured mini muffin tins and cook on the top shelf of the oven for 10-12 minutes, or until risen and golden. Remove the financiers from the oven and set aside for a few minutes.

Meanwhile, remove the chocolate orange cream filling from the fridge and allow it to come up to room temperature. Place the filling into a piping bag with a small fine plain nozzle and, while the financiers are still warm, pipe a small quantity into the centre of each one through the top. Serve immediately.

Garden Mint Ice Cream

This recipe was born out of having a glut of mint in the garden and Greg, the gardener, asking what he was to do with it all. I brought a big bunch of mint into the kitchen and played around a bit. I have a huge weakness for ice cream – we serve it in some shape or form nearly every day at Morston – so it wasn't surprising that I hit on the idea of making mint ice cream. This serves about 10 people, but I would always rather have too much than too little: it never gets wasted in my house! Anything chocolatey works well with this, as does Peach Melba on Almond Biscuit (*see* page 212).

Serves 10

570ml (1 pint) double cream

275ml (½ pint) full-fat milk

a large bunch of fresh mint,
  about 40g (1½ oz)

9 egg yolks

200g (7oz) caster sugar

Combine the cream and milk in a saucepan, place on a moderate heat and bring to just about boiling point. Add the mint, stir thoroughly and remove from the heat. Leave to infuse for at least 1 hour (any less and you won't get that great depth of mint flavour).

Gently reheat the mint-infused milk and cream mixture and remove the mint. In a large bowl, whisk the egg yolks and sugar together. Still whisking, carefully add the hot, mint-infused milk and cream.

Return the mixture to the pan and, over a low heat, stir continuously until the custard coats the back of a wooden spoon. Remove from the heat immediately and strain through a fine sieve into a jug. Leave to cool completely before churning to a soft consistency in an ice cream maker.

Serve immediately or freeze in a suitable container.

Lemon Ice Cream

I hope you will have a go at this recipe even though it's different from most ice creams in that it does not have a custard base. Although the method uses an ice cream machine, you can make really good ice cream without one. In this recipe, you simply place the mixture in a suitable container in the freezer, removing it every 20 minutes or so to mix it up really well until it is thoroughly frozen.

Serves 6

8 egg yolks

275g (10oz) caster sugar

juice of 4 medium lemons

zest of 1 lemon

570ml (1 pint) double cream

a sugar thermometer

Place the egg yolks in a large bowl and set aside.

Heat the sugar and lemon juice in a heavy-based saucepan over a low heat until the sugar has dissolved. Turn up the heat and, using a sugar thermometer, take the mixture to a temperature of 110C/230F (ie, just below the soft-ball stage).

Pour the hot sugar mixture on to the eggs yolks and, using an electric hand whisk, whisk thoroughly until the mixture cools and thickens. Stir in the lemon zest and cream.

Once cold, churn in an ice cream machine and serve immediately or freeze in a suitable container.

Malva Pudding

I think this recipe – given to me many years ago by my old boss John Tovey – has South African connotations. A real winter warmer of a pudding, it has the added attraction that it's also very boozy! Don't worry if the batter seems runny: trust me, if you follow the cooking instructions it will brown and set. Serve this pudding in small portions with more double cream, if liked, and let your guests come back for more. Believe me, they will, as this is classic comfort food.

Serves 8

2 eggs

450g (1lb) caster sugar

2 tbsp apricot jam

2 tsp bicarbonate of soda

a pinch of salt

425ml (¾ pint) milk

225g (8oz) plain flour, sifted

2 tbsp melted butter

2 tsp vinegar

For the sauce

175ml (6fl oz) double cream

110g (4oz) butter

175g (6oz) caster sugar

150ml (¼ pint) Cointreau

a well-buttered Pyrex dish, about 30 x 20cm and 7.5cm deep (12 x 8 inches and 3 inches deep)

Pre-heat the oven to 180C/350F/Gas 4.

Beat together the eggs and sugar till light and fluffy, then add the apricot jam and continue to beat. Once all the jam has been incorporated, beat in the bicarbonate of soda, salt, milk and flour. Finally, add the melted butter and vinegar and mix well.

Pour the batter into the Pyrex dish and place in the centre of the pre-heated oven. Bake for approximately 1½ hours (covering with foil if the pudding starts to brown too quickly), by which time the pudding should resemble a sponge and be set.

Meanwhile make the sauce. Place all the ingredients in a saucepan on a low heat, stirring occasionally until everything has melted and is incorporated. Keep warm.

Remove the pudding from the oven and pour over the hot sauce. Leave for a few minutes before serving.

Pancakes with Lemon Crème Patissière

Serves 8
(2 pancakes
per person)

For the lemon crème
patissière

510ml (18fl oz) milk

110g (4oz) caster sugar

1 vanilla pod, split

zest of 1 lemon

6 egg yolks

40g (1½oz) plain flour

For the pancakes

250g (9oz) plain flour

25g (1oz) caster sugar

a good pinch of salt

4 eggs

675ml (1 pint 3fl oz) milk

200ml (7fl oz) double cream

melted butter for frying the
  pancakes, and greasing the
  gratin dish

To serve

50g (2oz) soft brown sugar

300ml (½ pint) double cream

Make the lemon crème patissière. Place the milk in a saucepan with 50g (2oz) of the caster sugar, the vanilla pod and the lemon zest, then bring slowly to the boil. Meanwhile, place the egg yolks and remaining caster sugar in a bowl and gently whisk, adding the flour.

Pour the hot milk over the egg yolk mixture and beat well. Return the mixture to the saucepan and, using a wooden spoon, stir continuously over a low heat until the custard thickens and no longer tastes of flour. Strain the custard through a sieve into another bowl, place a piece of butter paper or clingfilm directly on to the surface and, when cool, place in the fridge until needed.

Make the pancake batter. Combine the flour, sugar and salt in a bowl, then add the eggs and 200ml (7fl oz) of the milk. Blend in a liquidiser, then strain the mixture through a sieve into a large jug. Stir in the remaining milk and the cream. Leave the batter to rest for at least 1 hour.

To cook the pancakes, heat a non-stick frying pan on a moderate heat. Brush the pan with the melted butter, then pour in a small ladleful of batter, quickly swirling it around to make a thin pancake.

When the underside of the pancake is just coloured, flip it over and cook the other side. Place the cooked pancake on a plate, then continue to cook the rest, placing a sheet of greaseproof paper between each one as you pile them up. You are aiming to make 16 pancakes in total.

Pre-heat the oven to 190C/375F/Gas 5 and generously butter a suitable ovenproof dish.

Spread a generous tablespoonful of the lemon crème patissière in the centre of each pancake, fold it in half, then fold it over again into the shape of an open fan. As you fill the pancakes, stand them in the buttered dish, pointed end downwards.

When all the pancakes are in the dish, sprinkle over the soft brown sugar and spoon over the double cream.

Warm the pancakes through in the oven for 10-15 minutes and then serve immediately.

Panettone Bread and Butter Pudding

This is about as good as bread and butter pudding gets and is another great pudding to serve at the table for its 'wow' factor. Although you can now buy panettone all year round, I tend to serve this at Morston from November through to March – in fact, it would be a good alternative to the traditional Christmas pudding.

Serves 8

500g (1lb 2oz) loaf of

  panettone

4 slices white bread, crusts

  removed

50g (2oz) unsalted butter,

  softened

25g (1oz) mixed peel

50g (2oz) sultanas

For the custard

12 egg yolks

110g (4oz) caster sugar

1 vanilla pod

425ml (¾ pint) milk

425ml (¾ pint) whipping

  cream

a well-buttered Pyrex dish,
about 25.5 x 23cm and
7.5cm deep (10 x 9 x
3 inches)

Begin by slicing the panettone into at least 8 slices of the same thickness as the bread. Butter all the slices. Arrange a layer of panettone, slices side by side, on the bottom of the dish. Sprinkle with half the mixed peel and sultanas, then add a layer of white bread slices, followed by the remaining mixed peel and sultanas. Add a final layer of panettone.

Make the custard. Whisk the egg yolks and sugar together in a bowl until well combined. Cut the vanilla pod lengthways and scrape out the seeds, then place these in a saucepan along with the milk and cream. Bring to the boil.

Pour the hot milk and cream over the egg yolks and sugar, whisk thoroughly and pass through a sieve into a jug. Skim off any excess bubbles from the surface to avoid them gathering on the surface of the pudding during cooking. Then, 20 minutes before cooking, pour the custard over the layers of bread and leave to soak.

While it is soaking, pre-heat the oven to 150C/300F/Gas 2.

Place the pudding in the pre-heated oven for about 1 hour, or until it is just set and brown on top (the middle should still be a little runny). Remove from the oven and serve straight away.

Passion Fruit Tart

This tart is a real winner, with a powerful passion fruit flavour. You can buy unsweetened passion fruit juice from specialist shops; alternatively, buy fresh passion fruit and scoop out the flesh and seeds – you will need about 30 fruit to produce 425ml juice. For some reason it is far easier to separate the seeds from the flesh if you whiz them in a food processor before passing the pulp through a sieve. This tart is best made on the day as the texture changes if you refrigerate it.

Serves 8

1 x 23cm (9 inch) flan ring, lined with sweet pastry (see page 24)

7 eggs

275g (10oz) caster sugar

425ml (¾ pint) passion fruit juice (see intro)

275ml (½ pint) double cream

To serve

Lemon Ice Cream (*see* page 202) or the pulp from 4 passion fruit

Pre-heat the oven to 180C/350F/Gas 4.

Cover the pastry-lined flan ring with baking parchment, fill with baking beans and place in the centre of the pre-heated oven. Bake 'blind' for about 30 minutes, or until the pastry just starts to colour.

Carefully remove the baking beans and parchment; if there are any cracks in the pastry, use leftover pieces of pastry or brush over beaten egg to fill them. It is important that the pastry is really well sealed. Return the pastry case to the oven for about 5 minutes. Leave to cool.

Turn the oven down to 140C/275F/Gas 1.

Whisk the eggs and sugar in a bowl, then whisk in the passion fruit juice and, finally, the cream. Pass this mixture through a sieve into a jug.

Place the pastry case on a baking tray in the centre of the oven, then carefeully pour in the passion fruit filling. Bake in the centre of the over for about 1 hour, by which time the tart should be just set round the edge but still fairly wobbly in the centre. Don't worry about this – the tart will set as it cools.

Allow the tart to cool before serving with Lemon Ice Cream (*see* page 202) or passion fruit pulp spooned alongside.

Peach Melba on Almond Biscuit

I imagine the original Peach Melba contained something along the lines of poached peaches, vanilla ice cream and raspberry purée, with sugared nuts sprinkled over. My version uses ripe peaches, home-made Garden Mint Ice Cream (*see* page 202), sugared nuts (bet you can't stop nibbling these!) and an almond biscuit base (*see* page 18), with lots of raspberry purée to complete the picture. You can make the components of this recipe well in advance, and simply assemble them when you are ready to serve.

Serves 6

For the sugared nuts

25g (1oz) pine kernels

25g (1oz) whole peeled
  almonds

25g (1oz) whole peeled
  hazelnuts

25g (1oz) chopped pecan
  nuts

110g (4oz) icing sugar

4 tbsp Grand Marnier

For the raspberry purée

225g (8oz) raspberries

juice of 1 lime

3 tbsp icing sugar

55ml (2fl oz) framboise
  (raspberry liqueur), optional

6 ripe, juicy peaches

sugar syrup (*see* page 214)

1 quantity Garden Mint Ice
  Cream (*see* page 202)

6 Almond Biscuits
  (*see* page 18)

For the sugared nuts, place all the ingredients in a large, heavy-based non-stick frying pan and, over the lowest possible heat, gently melt the sugar. Stir occasionally, being very careful once the sugar starts to caramelise. Take off the heat, place on a very lightly oiled tray and allow to cool. (These can be made in advance and kept for a few days in an airtight container.)

To make the raspberry purée, place all the ingredients in a liquidiser and blitz well. Pass the mixture through a fine sieve into a bowl and set aside.

Halve the peaches and place them in a pan of sugar syrup. Heat the syrup very gently, poaching the peaches until the skins slip off easily (it should take about 1-2 minutes).

Assemble the Peach Melba. Fill the centre of each peach with mint ice cream. Place an almond biscuit in the centre of each serving plate, then sit a peach on top. Scatter sugared nuts around the biscuits and, just before serving, drizzle raspberry purée over.

Real Custard (Crème Anglaise)

Serves at least 6

275ml (½ pint) double cream

150ml (¼ pint) full-fat milk

1 vanilla pod, split

6 egg yolks

110g (4oz) caster sugar

Pour the cream and milk into a heavy-based saucepan, then scrape in the vanilla seeds and the empty vanilla pod. Bring slowly to the boil, then set aside to infuse.

Whisk the egg yolks and sugar together in a large bowl. Gently re-heat the cream and milk mixture. As soon as it reaches boiling point, pour it on to the egg yolks and sugar, whisking all the time.

Return the custard to the saucepan and, over a low heat, stir continuously until the custard thickens enough to coat the back of a spoon.

Immediately remove the pan from the heat, then pass the custard through a fine sieve into a bowl. If you are not using it immediately, push a piece of clingfilm tightly down on top of the custard then another piece over the top of the bowl; this will prevent a skin from forming.

Sugar Syrup

This sugar or stock syrup is one of those standbys we always have in the fridge. Once you have made up a quantity, use it for any number of sorbets or for poaching fruit, as in Peach Melba on Almond Biscuit (*see* page 212). You can omit the vanilla pod if you wish; I have a thing about vanilla and enjoy seeing the seeds in any pudding. The easiest way to measure the ingredients is to take a jug and fill it to a given mark with sugar, then fill it up to the same mark with water.

Makes about 1 pint

caster sugar, measured to
  the 275ml (½ pint) mark in
  a measuring jug

275ml (½ pint) water

1 vanilla pod, split

juice of ½ lemon

Put the sugar and water into a saucepan. Scrape the seeds from the vanilla pod then add these to the sugar and water.

Over a low heat, allow the sugar to dissolve then bring it up to a light simmer for 10 minutes. Remove from the heat and allow to cool, then stir in the lemon juice.

This syrup will keep in the fridge for up to a week.

Raspberry or Mango Sorbet

Sorbets are easy to make and are a brilliant way of capitalising on the full flavour and colour of summer fruits. Raspberry has to be one of my favourites; it has a wonderful deep colour, and adding lemon juice really brings out the flavour. Serve it on its own, or use its colour to enhance other puddings. You could also use strawberries. Mango sorbet, too, is quite mouthwatering and truly exotic.

Serves 6-8

450g (1lb) raspberries or
really ripe mangoes
150ml (¼ pint) sugar syrup
(see page 214)
juice of ½ lemon, sieved

Blitz the fruit in a food processor or blender, then press it through a fine sieve into a jug.

Stir in the sugar syrup, tasting as you do so (you may not need to use all of it, the idea is to have a mixture which is sweet and yet bursting with the flavour of whichever fruit you choose). Finally stir in the lemon juice before churning in an ice cream machine.

White Chocolate Ice Cream

Serves 6

275g (10oz) good-quality
white chocolate, broken
into pieces
225ml (8fl oz) milk
425ml (¾ pint) double cream
8 egg yolks
75g (3oz) caster sugar
75ml (3fl oz) Bacardi
white rum

Melt the chocolate in a bowl over a pan of barely simmering water, making sure that the base of the bowl does not come into contact with the water.

Meanwhile, place the milk and double cream in a saucepan and bring slowly to the boil. In a bowl, whisk together the eggs yolks and sugar till they are thick and pale. Then, still whisking, slowly pour in the hot milk-and-cream mixture.

Transfer this mixture back to the saucepan and cook gently over a low heat, stirring continuously with a wooden spoon until the mixture is thick enough to coat the back of the spoon. Remove from the heat immediately. Leave to cool a little, then stir in the Bacardi, followed by the melted white chocolate.

Pass the mixture through a fine sieve and allow to cool completely before churning in an ice cream machine. Store in a container in the freezer.

Soufflé Rothschild (Apricot and Vanilla Soufflé)

I don't see why so many people are put off the idea of making a soufflé: what's more, most of the work can be done in advance, leaving just the egg whites to be whisked and folded in at the last minute. You must ensure the oven is pre-heated to the correct temperature – it's even better if the oven has a light so you can watch the soufflés rise without having to open the door. The apricot purée can be made from fresh apricots or a good-quality bought purée. The end result should be a soufflé that has risen at least 1cm (½ inch) above the rim of the ramekin. Go on, have a go.

Serves 10

75g (3oz) unsalted butter, softened

6 eggs, separated

175g (6oz) caster sugar, plus extra for sprinkling the ramekins

50g (2oz) plain flour

400ml (14fl oz) fresh apricot purée

seeds from 1 vanilla pod

icing sugar, for dusting

pouring cream, to serve

10 ramekins

Butter the ramekins with half the butter and place them in the fridge. When they have cooled, repeat the process with the remaining butter, sprinkle caster sugar inside the ramekins, shake to cover the sides, then return to the fridge again.

Make the soufflé base mixture. In a large bowl, gently whisk together the egg yolks, 110g (4oz) of the caster sugar and all the flour. Set aside.

Meanwhile, place the apricot purée and the vanilla seeds in a large saucepan and bring gently to the boil. Remove from the heat and pour over the egg, sugar and flour mixture, whisking it all together. Return the mixture to the large saucepan and, over a gentle heat, stir continuously to achieve a thick béchamel-type sauce.

Transfer this soufflé mixture to a large bowl. Cover the surface of the mixture with clingfilm to prevent it from drying out, then store at room temperature until needed.

Pre-heat the oven to 200C/400F/Gas 6 about 20 minutes before serving.

Whisk the egg whites in a food mixer at high speed till they form soft peaks. Still whisking, slowly add the remaining caster sugar. Then, using a slotted metal spoon, vigorously beat one-third of the egg whites into the soufflé base mixture before carefully folding in the remainder.

Fill the ramekins with the mixture, levelling it off with a palette knife. Then, run your thumb around the edge of each ramekin (this is important as it helps the soufflés to rise straight up). Place on a baking tray and cook on the top shelf of the oven for 8-10 minutes, by which time the soufflés will have risen dramatically!

Dust with icing sugar then, at the table, make a hole in the centre of each soufflé, and pour in some cream to serve.

Steamed Orange Sponge Pudding with Orange Cream Sauce

I wanted to include a steamed sponge pudding in this book and this one is a real blast from the past – made particularly good by its rich and decadent orange cream sauce. I like to use cubed cane sugar for the sauce because it dissolves more slowly to give a glossier, richer result. Also, it's well worth spending a little extra time creaming the butter and sugar together before adding the eggs as this will give you a much lighter sponge.

Serves 6

For the pudding

2 tbsp fine fresh
  breadcrumbs

5 tbsp golden syrup

zest and juice of 2 oranges

175g (6oz) unsalted butter,
  softened, plus extra for
  greasing

175g (6oz) caster sugar

3 eggs, lightly beaten

grated zest and juice of
  1 lemon

175g (6oz) self-raising flour,
  sieved

For the orange cream sauce

75g (3oz) cubed sugar

570ml (1 pint) double cream

grated zest and juice of
  2 oranges

900g (2lb) pudding basin

Grease the pudding basin with melted butter, sprinkle the inside with breadcrumbs, then place in the fridge to allow the butter to set.

Heat the golden syrup with the orange zest and juice in a small saucepan. Set aside to cool completely.

In a bowl, cream together the butter and sugar using a hand-held electric whisk, until thick and pale. Then, still whisking, slowly add the beaten eggs followed by the lemon zest and juice. Finally, carefully fold in the self-raising flour.

Take the pudding basin from the fridge and pour the cooled orange syrup into the bottom. Spoon the sponge mixture on top and cover with a circle of greaseproof paper. Next cover the basin with a double layer of tin foil or muslin, tying it securely with string.

Place the basin in the top of a double saucepan, covering tightly with the lid or foil and steam for about 1½ hours, topping the pan up with hot water as necessary. (The sponge is cooked when firm to the touch and will keep well for about 20 minutes off the heat as long as it is not opened.)

Meanwhile, make the orange cream sauce. Place the sugar and cream in a saucepan and slowly bring to the boil over a very low heat. Simmer until reduced by half, then add the orange zest and juice. Taste and, if necessary, reduce again until you have a rich, custard-like sauce.

To serve, run a sharp knife round the edge of the pudding basin and turn the pudding out on to a warmed plate. Serve with warm sauce.

Index